In the Mind
Of a Child

Book 1

K. Rareheart

In the Mind Of a Child – Book 1

Author: K. Rareheart

Copyright © 2025 K. Rareheart

The right of K. Rareheart to be identified as author of this work has been asserted by the author in accordance with section 77 and 78 of the Copyright, Designs and Patents Act 1988.

ISBN 978-1-83538-535-7 (Paperback)

Published by:
Maple Publishers
Fairbourne Drive, Atterbury,
Milton Keynes,
MK10 9RG, UK
www.maplepublishers.com

A CIP catalogue record for this title is available from the British Library.

All rights reserved. No part of this book may be reproduced or translated by any form or by any means, electronic or mechanical, including photocopying, recording or by any information storage and retrieval system without written permission from the author.

The views expressed in this work are solely those of the author and do not necessarily reflect the views of the publisher, and the publisher hereby disclaims any responsibility for them.

Introduction

This book is about a child, aged 13 months, called Brian. It follows him through his childhood and teenage years, as he shares his thoughts and feelings.

Brian begins his journey in a children's home, where he started life, and later grows up in his new home with a "Salvation Army Family."

Although, in the beginning, he was lost in a world of confusion, bewilderment, and deep sadness in his heart, he also experienced despair and anger over what was happening to him. He struggled to understand the reasons behind it all, and the things around him, for over half a century.

K. Rareheart

Chapter 1
My 1st Look at Life

It was in the middle of the night when I and my brother Kevin were rushed to the hospital with a rare disease. Kevin had been very ill for the first year of his life. This was the reason why Kevin and I were placed into care in the first place—because our real mum and dad could not cope with it all. However, Kevin and I didn't learn this until ten years later.

At the time, I was thinking, *What is going on? Who are all these people?* I wondered why they had come to see Mum and Dad. Then, I was put into a car and taken away.

We were placed in a children's home many miles away from our birthplace in the Midlands. By the time I arrived at the home, it was late at night, and I was fast asleep in the back of the car. Kevin was still in the hospital back in our hometown and was brought to the children's home some months later.

Something in my mind told me that this was not my real home. I felt an odd sensation within myself. When I woke up and looked around, I was confused by my surroundings. I wondered why I had been suddenly abandoned in this godforsaken, smelly, noisy place.

As I looked around to figure out where I was, I could make out the shapes of other cots in the early morning light. I vividly remembers the walls being two-tone green, with a wooden dado rail around the edges. The floor was made of polished wooden blocks, and the doors were large oak doors with rounded tops.

These are the kinds of thoughts that went through my mind throughout my childhood and into manhood.

During the night, I woke up, feeling bewildered in a large room filled with strange, dark shapes. I could hear whimpering coming from other parts of the room. I realised that I was no longer alone; I was in a room full of other children, lying in rows of cots. I was frightened, as I had no idea why I was in this place with forty or more children, all in their cots.

The children's home was in Darlington, Co. Durham. I had been in the home for just over 14 weeks when Kevin joined me at the home, Kevin was still quite ill, but getting better as the days and weeks went on. By the time Kevin was nearly 18 months old and I was just one year old, I had started to take notice of the things around me.

One day, I was introduced to another boy named Kevin. Little did I know at the time, I had a brother, also called Kevin, who had been in hospital for a rare disease. In the 1950s, this disease couldn't be cured. But by a stroke of luck, a doctor discovered a cure for

Kevin. Sadly, the doctor who cured Kevin later contracted the disease and passed away. RIP.

The next morning, after breakfast, I was put on the floor and left on my own. In the hallway, I saw a door open across from me. I crawled over and, as I got closer, I peered into the large room. The room was full of big, square shapes. As I got closer, I realised the shapes were big boxes full of toys. By the time I reached the door, I saw that some of the other children were already in the room, playing with the toys. I thought, *Maybe this isn't such a bad place after all.*

I went into the room and saw that the big boxes were filled with toys. There were toys all over the floor, and I found more children just like me—lost and alone.

I crawled over to one of the large toy boxes and pulled myself up, standing for the first time. I looked into the box and could hardly believe my eyes; it was full to the top with hundreds of toys. As I put my hand into the toy box and started pulling out some of the toys, a bigger child came over, grabbed the toy from my hand, and said, "Mine."

I tried again, but the boy did the same thing. Then I spotted a broken red car. As I pulled it from the box, the boy tried to take it from me again. But I held on tightly to the car. The boy continued to try to grab it, so I yanked the car away from him and hit him with it. The boy cried and left me alone after that.

Six months had now gone by, and I was 16 months old. I was sitting in the middle of the hallway floor, alone. I still didn't know that my brother Kevin was now well.

Still holding my broken red car, I looked around at my new home. I could see five massive steps leading down to the big oak front doors. I felt very uncomfortable; my nappy was leaking onto the floor. But one of the staff members came to my rescue and gave me a nice, clean, dry nappy.

Despite the time I had spent in the home, I was under the impression that no one wanted me. I felt very alone and unwanted, hurt by the thoughts running through my mind. People would come to the children's home, only to leave again. Sometimes they would take a child with them, but Kevin and I were always left behind.

Oh, how I craved the love of my mum and dad, who never came to get me. I couldn't understand why.

I felt so alone, sad, and unhappy. What had I done that was so bad that my parents would abandon me like this? My little heart was breaking.

Just a few weeks later, I was in the hallway when there was a knock on the door. One of the matrons went to answer it. When the door opened, there stood the Browne family from Darlington, a branch of the Salvation Army. They had come to visit the children's home for the afternoon. I was picked up by one of the Brownes and played with them all afternoon. It was great to have someone to play with, instead of being on my own all the time.

When it was time for the Brownes to leave, I didn't want them to go, but they left anyway, just like everyone else who had come to the home. I was alone again.

However, two of the girls who had visited that day went home and told their parents all about the little boy who was always alone in the hallway and how unhappy he was.

Just two weeks later, there was another knock at the door. This time, it was a middle-aged couple, along with the two Brownes. They had returned to learn more about the little boy they had seen alone in the hallway. The couple was taken into the office, while the Brownes played with me in the toy room.

It was there that they were told about my brother, Kevin, who had been in the hospital with a rare disease. The doctor who had treated Kevin had discovered a cure, but sadly, he had contracted the disease himself and had since passed away. However, Kevin was doing well now and should be out of the hospital in a few days, all being well.

The couple had already decided they would adopt or foster both of us. A couple of weeks later, they returned to the home.

I thought, *How are they back? Could this couple be my mum and dad, come to get me after all this time?*

Although I didn't fully understand what was happening or how it would affect me later in life, I had just learned that I wasn't alone after all. I had a brother, Kevin, who had just come out of the hospital a week before, although I didn't know what that meant.

The two Brownes, who had visited weeks ago, returned and spent time playing with Kevin and me until the couple came downstairs. The couple picked us both up and said, "Come on, boys, you're coming to live with us at our house."

And off we went. We were put into their car, an Austin A40. As we sat in the back with our new sisters, Joy and Hazel, we were whisked away to our new home. We had no idea what to expect.

I remember how frightened I was, venturing off into the unknown. But Joy and Hazel gave us both lots of hugs and kisses. I assumed Kevin must have been feeling the same way—frightened, confused, and excited all at once.

It was a cold February morning, and the ground was covered with a thick layer of snow. I had never seen snow before, and it was wonderful to see everything covered in it. As we all got into the car with our new Mum and Dad, we drove out of the countryside and into the town of Darlington, through the main high street, and just past a large park. Our new mum told us, "You're going to live near one of the biggest parks in Darlington. It's called South Park, and we'll take you to see it soon when the snow has cleared. It has the River Tees running through it, and it even has a skating rink!" At that point, I had no idea what she was talking about. I thought to myself, *Don't you know I'm not even two years old yet? And you expect me to understand all of this? Oh well, whatever.*

When we arrived at the house where we were going to live, we got out of the car, walked up the front garden path, and up the steps to the front door. On the other side of the door, in front of us, was a staircase, with a door on the right and one on the left. We were told that the door on the left was the front room, which we only used on Sundays. We were shown into the back room, which had a big dining table, a three-piece suite, and an open fireplace, as well as a door on the other side of the room that led into the kitchen. There was another door in the kitchen that led into the back garden.

We were then shown to our new bedroom, where there were new toys for us to play with, and none of them were broken. No one was going to take them away from us. However, I still got possessive over some of them, which was to be expected. I was very apprehensive and nervous about everything that had just happened. One minute, we were in a children's home, and now we were in a new home.

We were both picked up and shown our new garden out of the bedroom window. Then, we played with our new sisters, Joy and Hazel, for a while in our new bedroom with all of our new toys. I was still a bit confused and not at all sure about my new surroundings.

We all went outside to look around the garden. It was massive! The length seemed to go on as far as the eye could see, but we were only small at the time, so everything appeared super-sized to us. The excitement was all too much for me. There was just too much to take in all at once. But in time, it would all become clearer. For now, at least, I felt a bit happier than I had in the last 10 months or so—still confused, baffled, and definitely overwhelmed by the excitement of it all. But at the same time, I was afraid of what the next few months would bring, if they were anything like what I had already experienced in my short life.

We all sat down and had something to eat and drink with our new family. Kevin and I now had a new Mum and Dad, as well as two new sisters, Joy and Hazel, and countless cousins, aunts, and uncles we had yet to meet. I was very bemused by everything that was happening, but at the same time, I felt a sense of relief that I was no longer in the children's home. I was happy, but also very confused. I wasn't sure what to expect from my new surroundings and all the new things people were telling me. Not that I understood what it all meant or why this was happening to me. It was so hard to even try to understand, since I was so young at that time. I had no idea what to expect from my new life ahead.

After we had eaten, we were shown our new bedroom. We were carried up the stairs to the top. When we got to the top, there was a very short landing with one step on the left and one on the right. The one on the right led to a longer corridor that went to the bathroom, just next to our new bedroom. The door in front of us led into our new bedroom.

It all seemed so strange to be looking at our bedroom for the first time. There were only two beds in it, just for Kevin and me, and no other cots like there had been in the home. It felt so strange to be in a situation where I was looking at my new home for the first time. Everything was so quiet compared to the children's home, where there was constant crying or the banging of doors. In a strange way, peace and quiet were so nice to have at last.

I thought to myself that only time would tell. I felt a bit scared and apprehensive about my new home and how things were going to be from now on. Was life really going to be better, or was it going to be the same as it had been in the children's home? I felt so uptight, it was unbelievable. I felt all churned up inside, but at the same time, I was a bit happy. It was like I was shrinking inside myself, like a snail when danger came its way. Kevin, on the other hand, seemed to take to his new surroundings just like a duck to water.

Kevin held on to Joy, I think, to make sure Joy wasn't going to run away, just as I held on to Hazel. From then on, I was much closer to Hazel than I was to Joy. Hazel seemed to be much more loving than Joy was towards me. Joy always seemed to pay more attention to Kevin than to me, for some reason. But I wasn't too bothered at the time. As long as I was feeling loved, that was all that mattered. And from Hazel, I was getting love by the bucket load, and I loved every minute of it.

If this was to be my new life, then bring it on. I started to feel a little better about myself, but I was still very unsure of my new surroundings and the things yet to come. But I thought to myself that this was nicer than my life before my new home, and much better than the horrific start I had in my life so far.

Chapter 2
Discovering Our New Home

As I went into my new bedroom, I saw a big window looking out onto the back garden. The room had two single beds and the rest of the bedroom furniture. Under the window was a large toy box just for us, filled with toys that weren't broken. We got settled in, and Joy and Hazel played with us for some time to help us feel more relaxed about everything that had happened that day. We also looked out at the big garden through the window.

Hazel told us we could go out into the garden later. I could see down into the yard, where there was a slope leading up to the shed. Beyond the shed, the back garden stretched on for what seemed like hundreds of yards. Right at the far end, I could see the last row of houses and just a glimpse into the street over the back gate.

It was getting late, and after the most confusing day of my young life, I was exhausted. Our new mum came up and said, "It's bedtime now, boys. I'll leave the landing light on for you if you need to go to the loo in the night."

We got ready for bed, and she read us a bedtime story. Before the story was even halfway through, I had drifted off to sleep.

The bedroom curtains were closed, and the light was switched off, but the landing light stayed on with the bedroom door slightly ajar. After two or three hours, I woke up on my first night. It was a bit frightening. The room was dark, with just a little light shining through the partly open door. The birds outside had stopped singing, and there was an eerie silence.

It took me a long while to get back to sleep, but eventually, I drifted off again. I slept like I had never slept before, free from the noise of other children like it had been in the children's home.

As I woke up and opened my eyes in the early hours of the morning, I saw shapes in the room that hadn't been there the night before. There was a big one in the corner of the room that looked like someone standing still in the shadows. I didn't dare move, so I just shifted my eyes slowly around the room.

"Oh, God," I thought, "what's that in the middle of the wall near the window?" I felt so afraid. I just lay still until daylight began to creep in.

As the light grew brighter, I could see that the shape in the corner was just a lampshade on top of the wardrobe with an old hat perched on it. The other shape was just the reflection from the mirror on the chest of drawers. The curtains were slightly open, and daylight streamed through.

I could hear a strange noise coming from downstairs. It was just our new dad cleaning out the grates in the fireplaces, getting ready for later.

Meanwhile, I got up and looked out of the window, watching the birds in the garden for a while. When Kevin woke up, we watched the birds together, wondering what the day would bring.

Just then, Joy and Hazel came into our bedroom, still in their nighties. We all watched the birds in the garden together. Joy and Hazel told us the names of some of the birds having their breakfast.

Not long after, Mum came upstairs and told us it was time to get dressed and have breakfast. The four of us got ready and went downstairs. After breakfast, we went out into the garden to explore our new surroundings. The garden was 185 feet long, with a big lawn. Beyond the vegetable garden, there was a lilac tree, blackcurrant bushes, and gooseberry bushes.

Our new lives had just begun, and we would soon discover that many more nice things were yet to come. Our lives couldn't have been made any better.

Although we didn't realise it at the time, we were about to experience so much love in our young lives. Everything was so new to us, and we had no idea what to expect.

There were all sorts of questions racing through my mind. Was this new family just a stopgap until the next bad thing happened? Or was this the real deal? Was this going to be our new family for good—or at least until Kevin and I grew up?

We had no way of knowing how long this would last. All we could do was wait and see how our lives unfolded in this new home.

Joy and Hazel hugged us reassuringly and told us, "This is the first day of the rest of your new life with your new family."

They also told us about a big park down the road, with swings, slides, and much more to play on. They mentioned that we were going to have a picnic later, but for now, we could play in the garden with them.

By this time, I was walking on my own but still a bit wobbly. I didn't mind, as the girls were keeping an eye on us both. It was a big adventure. We had a great time in the garden while Mum and Dad prepared the picnic.

Before long, Mum called us inside and said it was time to go to the park. We all got into Mum's car for the short drive—it was too far for us to walk at our age, especially with a main road at the bottom of the street.

When we arrived at the park, we walked through big iron gates and down a path to a picnic area with tables and chairs, though we chose to sit on the grass. Mum spread out a blanket, and we all sat down. The food was lovely—sandwiches, cake, and fizzy drinks.

After eating, we explored the park with Joy and Hazel. Everything was so new and exciting that, for a while, I forgot about the children's home and the way we had lived without love or attention.

We went to a place called Children's Corner, where there were big cages filled with animals. The first cage had two albino peacocks, pure white and dragging their tails behind them. We stood watching for a long time, waiting for them to fan out their tails. When they did, it was a wonderful sight.

Next, we saw genets playing in another enclosure. There were all sorts of birds and small animals in this part of the park.

As we came out of Children's Corner, we heard music in the distance. Mum told us it was coming from the skating rink, and we would go there later.

We walked past the bowling greens and through the gardens to the clock tower, then on to the skating rink. We sat and watched as people skated below us on roller skates. Dad told us how he used to skate when he was younger and promised we could try it when we were older.

We had a fantastic day. The girls told us we had only seen a quarter of the park and that a fair came once a year—but we'd have to wait until next year.

We all got back into the car, and we were shown around town from the comfort of it. We were shown the Cattle Market and where Dad worked at the railway station goods yard. Kevin and I were both plum tuckered out after a day in the park and fell asleep in the car.

Our new mum and dad, Hazel and Joy, belonged to the Salvation Army and were very active in it. Mum played the organ, Dad played in the band, and Hazel and Joy were in the Singing Company, which is like a young people's choir in a church. Kevin and I were too young to join in, so we just attended meetings on Sundays and other events during the week.

Mum went to the Home League, and at the end of the meetings, we all had tea and cakes. I had juice and cakes. As the two new additions to the family, we were spoilt rotten by all the other women in the Salvation Army. Kevin and I had a whale of a time, lapping it up.

Over the next four to six months, things started to relax and settle down, and we got into a routine. We were happier than we had ever been in months. Six months later, Mum told me that it was going to be my birthday soon.

I thought to myself: *Birthday? What was that all about? A birthday for me?* I had never heard of such a thing before. I was about to find out in the coming days. It was to be my second birthday, but I didn't know what it meant to have one.

Two days later, that evening, Hazel and Joy told me that the next day was my birthday.

"You'll get something called presents," they said. "You'll see in the morning."

The mind boggled. Still, I guessed it would be alright—I'd find out soon enough. I felt puzzled and confused again, and my mind was going into overdrive, thinking all sorts of things. Did this mean we were going to be sent away? Or was it something else?

I thought about it for hours. The question in my mind was: *Is it going to be nice or something very bad?* Had Kevin and I done something wrong in the last couple of weeks? A few hours later, Hazel and Joy noticed I was worrying about something.

The morning of my third birthday arrived. It happened just as Hazel and Joy had said. Sure enough, at the end of my bed was one present. After breakfast, I was given the rest. I now felt a sense that I did have a new home. Yet, deep down inside, there was a sense of emptiness I couldn't explain or shake off. I wouldn't understand it fully for many years to come—I was simply too young to work it out for myself at that time.

I was beginning to understand quite a lot about life now that I was a bit older and had a mind of my own. I enjoyed the rest of my birthday and learned that birthdays weren't the big, nasty things I had imagined.

First, they asked me what I thought a birthday meant.

I told them, "I thought it meant Kevin and I were going to be sent away."

By the time I said it, I had tears running down my face and was so choked up I could hardly speak. Hazel said, "Come here and sit on my knee." She gave me a big hug and said, "No, you've got it all wrong. That's not what happens at all. Now, dry your eyes, and let me tell you both what will happen on your birthdays."

She continued, "First, when you get up in the morning on your birthday, you'll find a present at the bottom of your bed—a bit like Christmas. But there will only be one. Then, when you come down to breakfast, you'll be treated very specially because it's your birthday. After breakfast, you'll have the rest of your presents, and that's all that will happen. You're both here to stay for good, and we will never, ever send either of you away. We are your family now, okay?"

The next morning came, and after breakfast, I was given my birthday presents. I felt a new feeling for the first time—something I couldn't quite identify. My heart was pounding like it never had before. I felt a strange warmth inside me with my new family sometimes, but I also felt something stopping me from loving them back.

Although I didn't mean to, I was starting to block my new family off because of the confusion in my mind. Maybe this would pass in time as I got older.

Hazel and Joy could see that I was in another place in my mind. I looked very confused and often sat alone, my thoughts far away. Although I now had a new family, and they were very kind people, I still felt like nobody's child. I had no real mum or dad to give me the love, hugs, and kisses I desperately wanted.

I couldn't understand what I had done that was so bad for my real parents to put Kevin and me into a children's home in the first place. I often felt so alone, even though I was getting more love than I could have ever had from my own parents.

I just didn't understand how different things were from being with my real mum and dad. Maybe, in time, I would be able to show my new parents the love I now held in my heart and within myself and forget all about my real parents. Only time would tell.

Maybe I was just being silly and overreacting to the love I was receiving from my new family. There was a lot of love coming my way, but I wasn't experiencing it in the way I was supposed to. Something in my own mind was stopping me from accepting that the love I was being shown was true and genuine. I was simply too young and confused to understand.

One day, Hazel came over to me in the garden, gave me a hug, and said, "Everything will be just fine—you wait and see. We all love you, and we'll always be here for you both, forever. So don't look so sad, okay? You'll be happy with us, and we'll always look after you."

Sometime later, Joy came over and told me it would soon be my second birthday. I thought to myself, *Birthday? What was that all about?* I had never heard of a birthday before. Hazel and Joy explained it all to me—what it meant to have a birthday.

They said, "Once a year, on the same day you were born, you get a year older, and it's called a birthday. You get presents just like at Christmas, but only you get them, and the family sings 'Happy Birthday' to you."

For the first time, I began to understand the concept of birthdays—and what they really meant.

Chapter 3
Our 1ˢᵗ Christmas

It was to be my first Christmas in our new home, and December was just two months away. All the shops were putting up their Christmas decorations. One day, we went shopping, and as I got into the car, Mum said, "Boys, do you know what Christmas is really all about?"

I said, "No," with a puzzled look on my face.

Mum said, "Well, we'll have to tell you all about it, but I think it can wait until we get back home later."

Just then, Dad came out of the house, got into the car, and off we went.

When we got to town, Mum parked the car in a car park, and we walked to the shops from there. We went into a lot of shops and bought plenty of things for Christmas, returning to the car a few times to drop things off. Then we went to a restaurant. It was the first time Kevin and I had ever been in a restaurant, and we were very excited. We had to be on our best behaviour.

As we entered, Dad said we could order anything we wanted from the menu. We sat down and looked at the menu, but I realised I was having trouble reading it. To avoid admitting this to Mum and Dad, I chose the same thing as Kevin.

After dinner, I asked, "Mum, what is Christmas all about then?"

Mum replied, "Well, many years ago, when the world was created by God, who lives in Heaven far beyond the stars, He wasn't very happy with the way mankind had gone astray from what He first intended. So, He sent His only son to be born of the Virgin Mary, wife of Joseph from Jordan. God sent a message through the Archangel Gabriel to shepherds, three kings, and three wise men, as well as to all of Judea and the world, about the baby who was to be called Jesus Christ, the Son of God."

While I understood most of what Mum explained, I was even more baffled than before. Mum reassured me that, over time, I'd come to understand it all.

She added, "Nowadays, we celebrate by giving and receiving presents on the birthday of Jesus, which is called Christmas Day—25th December each year. That's when Father Christmas comes down every chimney in the world on Christmas Eve in his red suit."

We had seen Father Christmas in a shop earlier that day.

On the way home, Kevin and I wondered aloud, "How does he do it all in one night? That's a lot of chimneys. Doesn't his red suit get black with soot?"

On Christmas Eve, we left a mince pie and a glass of ginger cordial for Father Christmas, as our parents didn't drink alcohol. Then we went off to bed. Mum and Dad told us that if we didn't go to sleep, Father Christmas wouldn't come and leave us presents. We tried our best to sleep, but I couldn't stop thinking about what Mum had said earlier. How would Father Christmas come down in our house? We had three chimneys—one in the front room, one in the back room, and one in Mum and Dad's bedroom. And how on earth could a big fat man get down such a small chimney pot? Eventually, I drifted off to sleep.

I woke up a couple of times during the night to check if Father Christmas had been, but each time, he hadn't. Finally, I couldn't keep my eyes open any longer and fell asleep.

On Christmas Day, Kevin and I woke up to find stockings full of toys and gifts at the bottom of our beds. Unsure if we were allowed to open them, we pretended to stay asleep until Joy and Hazel, still in their nightclothes, came into our room and woke us up.

Hazel told us, "Every Christmas morning, we always go into Mum and Dad's bedroom to open the presents in our stockings. Then we have breakfast and head to the Christmas morning service at the Army."

We followed Hazel and Joy into Mum and Dad's room. All four of us climbed onto the bottom of their bed, where a long pillow called a bolster lay, and opened the presents in our stockings.

After that, we went downstairs for breakfast. Once we were dressed, we attended the short Christmas morning service at the Salvation Army, which only lasted half an hour. Then we returned home for Christmas dinner.

We had a huge turkey with all the trimmings. After dinner, we sat by the Christmas tree in the front room—only used on Sundays—and opened the rest of our big presents.

Kevin and I had never seen so many presents before in our lives. There were all sorts of wonderful things, and we were overwhelmed. For the first time, I started to feel loved. We had great fun playing for the rest of the day, right into the evening. At one point, I even fell asleep among the toys and woke up with the imprint of a car wheel on my face.

That night, we went to bed absolutely exhausted. The next day, Boxing Day, we played with our toys all day. It was a wonderful time in our lives. There was so much love coming from our new family. We felt wanted and cherished for the first time, and it was an unforgettable feeling.

Despite the joy, I struggled to feel completely part of the family as Kevin did. I often kept my feelings to myself, becoming a strong, silent type. I observed everything around me but found it hard to join in. There were occasional times when I interacted with the family and their friends in the Salvation Army, but most of the time, I preferred to play alone.

Deep down, it felt like something inside me was missing, holding me back from fully loving my new Mum, Dad, and sisters, Joy and Hazel. I got along better with Hazel than Joy, as she seemed friendlier toward me, but I couldn't see that the whole family loved us both equally.

This inability to connect fully stemmed from my early experiences of being taken from my biological parents and placed in a children's home. Although our new parents treated us all the same, I couldn't open up to them. It felt like an emotional block I couldn't overcome, no matter how hard I tried.

I often wondered what my biological parents looked like. That thought stayed with me for a long time, surfacing whenever I felt down or depressed. Over time, it receded into the back of my mind but never truly went away.

This loneliness became part of me, a defence mechanism I developed to cope with life's challenges. Although it made me feel isolated, it also gave me mental strength and determination to achieve my goals.

Even now, that sense of loneliness lingers. It's something I've carried with me since those early days, shaping who I am today.

Chapter 4

My 4th Birthday

Going back to 1957, when I was four years old, I got a tricycle with a boot for my birthday. Kevin already had one from six months before. By this time, we were allowed out on our new bikes, but we were told not to go too far—just to stay in the back streets and alleys. The road Mum mentioned was only a side street, and not many cars passed through.

On my first time out to play, we went through the back gate, up the three steps, and into our back street, which was a dead end. Off we went down the back street to the other end, over the junction, across the road, and into a network of back alleys. From there, we could explore all sorts of places in our area. We found some chalk, and as we ventured further, we used it to mark arrows showing our way back.

As we wandered through the alleys, we met two girls who became very good friends—Barbara and Anita. We called them "Babes" and "Nits" for short. Together, we roamed all over the place. They even showed us how to get into the back of the cattle market by going through the alleys, avoiding the main roads. Babes and Nits lived on the main road, and their parents, who were German, were quite strict—similar to our new parents.

All summer, we played on our tricycles in the alleys and back streets. One day, we were allowed to visit the big park just over the main road at the bottom of our street, and Babes and Nits came with us.

When we got to the park gates, there was a gigantic grassy field in front of us. It was so vast we couldn't see the other side, only trees in the distance. There wasn't a path at this entrance, but beside the gate was a black path covered with ash from the steelworks' fires, so it was called the Black Path. We went down the path, leaving a dust trail behind us. On our right was a large concrete-covered pipe, and behind it were weeds and bushes. On our left stood black, spiky metal railings.

At the other end of the field, we found another gate. Ahead was a path leading over the river and into the town and market, but we turned left into the park. About halfway down the path, we came to a place called Pat's Corner. There were big cages with animals like guinea pigs, rabbits, peacocks, and many others. We hadn't even explored the entire park yet.

The park was divided into two halves. In the first half, where we were, a river flowed all the way through, under the main road, and into the second half. It led to a place called the Seven Falls, named for the seven small waterfalls at the park's far end. The waterfalls weren't very high, but they were still intimidating as water crashed onto the rocks below and rushed through the rapids.

In our half of the park, there was a roller-skating rink, a play area with swings, slides, a Witches' Hat, and climbing frames of various sizes. We had a wonderful time playing tag and seeing who could swing the highest.

We got lost a couple of times but eventually found our way back home.

The next day was my fourth birthday, and Mum and Dad told us there was going to be a special surprise for the family. They wouldn't say what it was, so we had to wait until the next day to find out.

To our delight, a black-and-white television arrived! After tea, we watched the new TV. It took quite a while to warm up and tune in, but we were fascinated. Not many people had one in those days. We watched children's programmes until 6 o'clock, when the news came on, and then we went to bed.

At bedtime, Joy and Hazel came into our bedroom, as they always did, to give us a kiss goodnight. This time, they put a finger to their lips and whispered, "Shush, listen. We're going to have a midnight feast tonight, so don't be surprised when we come and get you at the stroke of midnight."

Sure enough, at midnight, Joy and Hazel, still in their nighties, woke us up for the feast. We all sneaked downstairs into the kitchen, where we gorged on cakes, biscuits, pop, and sandwiches. By the end, we were all full to bursting. It was great fun! We crept back to bed and quickly fell asleep. I remember thinking, Boy, I'm going to explode!

The next morning, none of us—Joy, Hazel, Kevin, or I—could finish our breakfast. Mum must have guessed what had happened because she said with a smile, "Oh dear, I hope you're not all coming down with a tummy bug." She didn't mention it again, but I'm sure she knew.

Later that day, we went back to the park to explore the second half and see where the river went. We walked across the field to the trees and heard music coming from the other side. Following a path through the trees, we found the roller-skating rink, full of people having fun. Past the rink, we saw a white tower through more trees. It turned out to be the clock tower Mum had told us about, and we used it as a landmark.

Continuing past the bowling greens, we followed the river. It was quiet at first but became louder as we walked. Soon, we reached a wide concrete waterfall with a footbridge over the river. Kevin and I threw twigs upstream to watch them go over the falls and smash onto the rocks below.

On our way back, we took a wrong path and ended up in a different playground with swings, slides, and three roundabouts. Eventually, we found our way to the gates and the other end of the

Black Path. We raced along, leaving a dust trail behind us. It had been a perfect day—a real adventure!

When we got home, we told Mum and Dad all about it. Mum said, "Did you know that park is three miles by five miles across? What a great place to play!"

We often returned to the park, sometimes with Babes and Nits. It was a wonderful place to explore, though we learned to avoid the rough boys from a place called Scrnpark. They were always looking for trouble, and we usually came off worse when we encountered them. Still, the park remained a safe haven for us and a place of endless adventures.

One summer, there was a circus in the park. Mum and Dad told us to visit it one Saturday afternoon. When we arrived at the park, we could see the Big Top and loads of other attractions. There was a big ring of side stalls and all sorts of activities going on. We had a look around and then went into the Big Top to see the show. We sat in the third or fourth row from the front, so we had a good view of everything that was happening.

First, the ringmaster came in to introduce all the acts. The elephants came on first, standing on big balls and manoeuvring over various obstacles. Between acts, the clowns performed. They had a car that fell apart, which was very funny. Then, there was a flurry of activity as they brought in the giant cages for the lions, tigers, and two black panthers.

When the setup was complete, the lion tamer entered the cage. He gave a signal for the doors to be opened, and the crowd fell silent as the lions strolled into the ring. They jumped through hoops and performed a few tricks, as did the tigers. The black panthers strutted into the ring, but something seemed off—they didn't want to do anything. However, it turned out to be part of the act. We had a fantastic time at the circus that day.

Mum told me that next year, when I turned five years old, I would be starting school, but she said we'd cross that bridge when we came to it.

A couple of months later, Mum and Dad dropped the biggest bombshell of my life. Kevin and I were playing with the dog in the garden when Mum called out of the kitchen window, "Boys, can you both come in? Your dad and I have something to tell you."

Kevin said to me as we walked back down the garden path, "It sounds like we're in trouble for something."

I said, "But we haven't done anything wrong—at least, I haven't!" Kevin couldn't think of anything either.

We went inside, looking puzzled. Mum told us we hadn't done anything wrong, so we shouldn't worry. She asked us to sit on the sofa in the front room, saying she and Dad would join us in a moment. Kevin and I exchanged nervous glances as we walked into the room.

"The front room," Kevin muttered. "We only use this room on Sundays. Something's not right."

Just then, we heard Mum and Dad come in from the kitchen.

"Well, boys," Mum began, "we think it's time to tell you something very important. It happened four years ago, and up until now, you've both been too young to understand. But we believe you're old enough now."

Mum continued, "When you were little, you both lived in a children's home. I don't expect you to remember it. Do you?"

Kevin shook his head, but I said, "Yes, I remember. We lived in a big house before we came here."

"You're right, Brian," Mum said. "That big house was the children's home. The reason you were both put into care wasn't because of anything you did. It was because your real mum and dad couldn't cope at the time—especially with Kevin's illness and you being such a young baby."

She went on to explain that Kevin had been very ill as a baby with a rare disease, which he later recovered from. Tragically, the doctor who treated him contracted the disease and died.

"That's why you ended up in the children's home," Mum said. "One day, two girls from the Darlington Browns visited the home. When they came back, they told us about a little boy sitting alone, playing with a broken toy. That was you, Kevin. Your dad and I visited the home to see for ourselves, and that's when we found you just out of hospital."

Mum then explained, "We aren't your real parents; we're your adoptive parents. That means we're legally your parents, and you'll live with us until you're grown up and ready to start a life of your own."

This was the biggest shock of my life. Kevin seemed to take it all in stride, but I was completely devastated. I didn't say anything at the time, but my mind was in turmoil. I'd known for a while that something didn't feel quite right, but I couldn't figure out what it was. Now that the truth was out, I felt overwhelmed.

When Mum asked us what we thought, Kevin said, "I'm happy," and I said, "Yes," but I didn't mean it. I felt torn up inside but didn't let it show.

Over the next week, I thought about it constantly. One day, I went to the park alone to play. When I got there, the play area was empty, so I climbed to the top of the climbing frame. Sitting there, I felt so alone, so lost in my thoughts, that I nearly lost my balance and fell. Luckily, I managed to steady myself just in time.

As I climbed down, I resolved to try to love Mum and Dad. But as I walked home that day, I knew it wouldn't be easy to fool them about how I really felt.

Chapter 5
1st School Days

I went to school for the first time on a cold September morning, and I did not want to go. I had this crazy notion in my mind that my new mum was trying to get rid of me, just like my real mum had done shortly after I was born. I'd forgotten everything Hazel had told me just after Christmas about when she went to school for the first time.

The school I was going to was quite a walk from our home. As we walked down the road, we crossed the street where Babes and Nits lived, continued down a long road, passed under the railway bridge, and crossed the unmanned train crossing. We walked past the steelworks and on to the next main road, eventually reaching the school.

When we arrived at the school gate, we stopped for a moment. I looked at the size of the playground—it seemed as vast as a park, at least five miles square to my eyes, though of course, it wasn't nearly that big.

Mum, still holding my hand, said, "Come on then, it's time to go into school."

I didn't want to go. I kicked and fought, but off we went anyway.

When we reached the huge green double doors, a teacher met us and grabbed my other hand, pulling me in. Mum shut the doors behind me, thinking I was safely inside, but my fingers were still caught in the door.

I had never felt such pain in my life as I did then. With a scream so loud, I nearly deafened both the teacher and myself. The teacher, however, just told me to stop being such a baby and led me to the classroom.

My fingers throbbed like mad, but after a while, the pain eased, and I started to feel a bit better. Once I was in the classroom, standing in the doorway with tears running down my face, I dried my eyes on my sleeve and sat down with all the other kids who were starting school that day for the first time. After that, I was all right.

For some reason, I always seemed to be happier with animals than with people. Our dog at home, for example—I could understand what animals wanted or were asking for faster than anyone else. Quite why that was, I didn't know at the time.

Even Babs and Nits' guinea pigs seemed to feel safer with me than with Kevin, Babs, or Nits. They all got bitten at one time or another, but I never did. I was the same with wild animals.

For the next year, I went to school on my own most of the time, though sometimes I went with Kevin. I liked it better that way. I still seemed to prefer my own company over being with other people.

But that sense of having a gift, as some people had called it before, was soon to change in the next year.

Dog Attack

A year later, by then, I was going to school on my own as always. I knew the way off by heart. But one morning, as I was walking to school, I passed an Old English Sheepdog on the other side of the road. There was no owner in sight. It wasn't long before I realised the dog was following me, keeping to the opposite side of the road, just behind me. I could still see it in the corner of my eye.

The dog suddenly crossed the road. I stopped to stroke it and give it a fuss, but when I turned around, the dog stopped and growled at me, baring its teeth. Feeling uneasy, I turned and started walking away, heading towards school. I picked up my pace, and the dog did the same.

I started to panic when I noticed the dog was drooling at the mouth. *This isn't good*, I thought, trying to figure out what to do. I spotted a wall nearby and decided I could jump onto it to get out of the dog's reach and shout for help. It seemed like a good idea at the time, but it turned out to be a mistake. The wall, which was only shoulder-height, was just too high for me.

As I tried to jump up onto the wall, the dog bit me in the back of my leg and wouldn't let go. In desperation, I kicked the dog with my other foot. Thankfully, it let go and ran off yelping. After a short time, the dog disappeared down the street.

Across the road was the steelworks. Still perched on the wall, I realised I was losing a lot of blood from my leg. A steelworker came over to see what had happened. Seeing my injury, he picked me up, wrapped my leg tightly to stem the bleeding, and took me home. Mum rushed me to the hospital for treatment.

All the while, I kept thinking, *I'll get that dog back for this one day.*

The Bull in the Market

During the summer holidays that year, we played a lot with Babes and Nits, sometimes in the outhouse where they kept their guinea pigs. One day, we took a walk up the back alley behind their house, all the way to the top end. In the corner, there was a telegraph pole that we could climb to get into the cattle market. Once over the wall, we'd jump into the sandpit and head into the market.

Sometimes, after market day, there were still animals left in the pens, and we'd go to see them. One time, as we entered through the usual way near the slaughterhouse, we found a big, fat, bushy-looking bull with enormous horns in a pen, waiting to be slaughtered.

We went up to the gate to get a closer look. As the bull spotted us, it scraped its front hoof on the ground and looked ready to charge at the gate. We quickly backed away.

Sitting in the sandpit, we decided to set the bull free. *Big mistake.*

Thinking it was cruel to kill animals, we returned to the pen. The bull was on the far side, so we opened the gate and ran like the wind back to the sandpit, climbing onto the wall to watch what would happen next.

At first, the bull just stood there, staring at the open gate. After a moment, it scraped its hoof again and charged out of the pen, heading down into the cattle market.

We followed at a safe distance to see what it would do. For a short while, we lost sight of it, but when we turned a corner into the cattle sheds, we found it again. The bull had its way with some cows that were chained up in the shade. Realising it was time to leave, we hurried back to the sandpit, keeping an eye out to make sure the bull wasn't following us.

Just as we reached the sandpit, we heard a noise—the bull was behind us! We scrambled up the sand pile and onto the wall, just in time. The bull tried to follow us but sank into the sand. We quickly climbed back over the wall, down the telegraph pole, and into the back alley, sighing with relief as we headed home.

When Kevin and I got back, Mum asked if we'd been in the cattle market again. We both said, "Oh no, Mum."

Mum replied, "What's that then?" pointing at the backs of our jeans, which were still stained with cow dung. *Caught out again.*

Paddling in the River

The next day, we went to the large park and along the riverbanks, as we often did. We had been told many times not to play in the river because it ran quite fast, but we couldn't resist. With our shoes off, we waded into the shallows where we often went fishing with our nets, catching minnows and other small fish.

One day, while we were fishing, a newspaper reporter came and took our photo for *The Northern Echo*.

A week or two later, after playing in the park, we got home, and Mum asked if we had been paddling in the river. "No, Mum," we said. "We haven't. It's too dangerous."

Mum replied, "I'll ask you both one more time. Have you been paddling in the river? Tell me the truth!"

We both insisted, "No, we haven't."

Mum then held up the newspaper, pointing at the photo of us paddling in the river. "What's this, then? Scotch mist?"

We were both sent to bed without tea for lying. *Caught out again.*

The next day, we apologised profusely for telling lies. Mum told us, "Liars will always get caught out, every time. So don't do it again."

Chapter 6

Snowed in at Christmas

Christmas was now just three months away, and I knew it was such a happy time of the year and what it really meant to the family as a whole. But this Christmas was going to be different. Now, I knew the truth about where I had come from at the beginning of my life. So much of what I thought I could remember from when I was a baby turned out to be true and had happened pretty much as I recalled. My innermost feelings started to make more sense than ever before.

That Christmas week, it snowed so heavily that we didn't go to the Christmas Day family service. The snowstorm was relentless. Both Kevin and I had received sledges as presents and were eager to try them out, but we had to wait until Boxing Day morning. By then, the snow had stopped, and after breakfast, we got ready to head outside.

What we hadn't accounted for was the two steps leading down into the back yard. As we stepped out of the back door, we disappeared into a 14-foot drift of snow piled up in the yard. We came back into the house looking like two abominable snowmen.

Disappointed, we realised we'd have to wait for the snow to clear before we could properly play outside.

For a week, we were stuck playing indoors until the snow melted enough to let us outside with our new sledges. When we finally ventured out, we had hours of fun in the garden, throwing snowballs and building a giant snowman in the middle of the grass.

As the days went on, the snow slowly melted, turning the garden into mud. But that didn't stop us. All the kids went outside and made the biggest snowman we could from the remaining snow. By the time we were done, we were covered in mud. This led to an all-out mud fight—it was still the Christmas holidays, after all!

Later, Hazel, Joy, Kevin, and I had a long hot bath together to clean up. Those were the good old days, long before things changed so much. We were so filthy that the bathwater had to be changed twice! Afterward, we went back downstairs for a nice cup of soup to warm ourselves up. Kevin and I thought Mum and Dad would be furious about how muddy we'd gotten, but they just saw the funny side of it all.

Shortly after Christmas, in the New Year, the whole family went into town to get new school uniforms in preparation for my first experience at school. At the time, I felt great about it. But as the day approached, I began to feel increasingly nervous. I didn't want to let the family see how I felt, so I tried to hide it. I thought I was doing a good job, but Hazel noticed something was bothering me.

She came over and took me upstairs to play for a while. Hazel and I had a long talk. She told me all about her first day at school and how nervous she'd been. She reassured me by sharing how she soon made lots of new friends. Her words made me feel much more confident about starting school in four months.

Chapter 7

Holiday in London

In our last year in Darlington, we were taken on holiday to the place where Dad was born—London. We were going for two weeks, and we were going by train for the first time. Many times, Kevin and I had gone to Darlington train station to watch the steam trains coming and going, but we had never been on one. We had a holiday in a railway coach the year before, but that's not like going on a real steam train.

The big day came, and Kevin and I couldn't wait. We were very excited as we boarded the train. When we arrived at the station and got onto the platform, just a few minutes later, Dad said, "Look, boys, down the track." We both looked down the track, and in the distance, we could see a small train getting bigger and bigger as it got closer. As it pulled up at the station and chugged past us, the smoke filled the station, and we couldn't see a thing, just for a few moments. It was hard to breathe for a couple of seconds. We all got on the Flying Scotsman and chugged out of Darlington Station. We could see the smoke billowing out of the engine's chimney as we went around the bends in the track, and off we went on our long journey from Darlington to London. The carriage we were in had tables, and we played games and looked out of the window, watching the countryside go by.

When we got close to London, Dad said, "Look out of the window, boys. Soon you'll see the skyline of London." We looked out of the window, and a few minutes later, we saw in the distance the shape of a large building. As we got closer to the City of London, it got bigger and bigger. Dad pointed out some of the buildings and named them all. Then Dad said, "Look, boys, there's London Bridge. We'll be going over the River Thames soon."

I thought that London was massive, and as we got closer to the River Thames, it just seemed to get wider and wider. I was getting very nervous as we were just going over London Bridge. It was really wide, and I was hoping that the bridge would hold the weight of the train. Just then, I saw another train coming from London over the same bridge, and then I knew we would be okay. And we, of course, made it over to the other side of the Thames. (Silly me.)

We arrived at the station at dinner time. We got off the train and got into a London taxi to the hotel. Once we had sorted ourselves out at the hotel, we all went out for a meal at a restaurant Dad knew. There, we had a big slap-up meal.

After that, we went out to see some of the sights in London. We went to see the famous Tower of London and Buckingham Palace, where the Queen lived. I said to Dad, "Doesn't the Queen get lost in there?" Dad said, "No, she knows that house like the back of her hand." Then we saw the Changing of the Guards at Buckingham Palace, and then we all went back to the hotel for our first cream tea and cakes. After tea at the hotel, we went out to see London's lights at night, and on the way back to the hotel, we went to a milk machine. The milk from the machine was only 6d a pint and was icy cold. We had one every night before we went to bed.

We saw many sights in London. We went to Madame Tussauds, which was a bit spooky, and the wax museum was very realistic. We also went to The Salvation Army Trade in London. We had been on holiday in London for 9 days and nights, when on the 10th night we went to the milk machine for our nightcap. But when I started to drink my milk, I got a terrific toothache. I told Mum and Dad, and they had a look. Dad said, "It looks like you might have the start of an abscess behind your front tooth, Brian. No more icy cold milk for you out of the machine." This was 4 days before we were going back home.

When we got back home, Mum took me to see the dentist the next day. The dentist took one look and confirmed what Dad had said while we were on holiday. It was an abscess, and it was quite bad. He said if he didn't lance it straight away to get the poison out, it would burst on its own and then I'd be in big trouble. So that's just what he did, and I was relieved to have all that poison taken out of my mouth.

I remember he filled two large syringes full of the poison. After the dentist had finished, my mouth wasn't so sore, and a couple of days later, my mouth had gone back to its normal size. I could drink as much cold drinks as I wanted again.

Kevin kept taking the mick out of me because of what had happened on holiday. Mum told Kevin to stop being so nasty to me and that he wouldn't like it if it was him instead of me. She said that's not the way he had been taught and that it was not the Christian way. Dad said, "Remember, Kevin: what comes around, comes around."

Well, sure enough, just two weeks later, Dad's words came true. Kevin, Babs, Nits, and I went roller skating on the park's roller skating rink. It was only 1/- for as long as you could stand up on your skates. We had been enjoying ourselves for about 2½ hours when Kevin started to show off to Babs, Nits, and me. He was showing how fast he could go and how he could spin around on the spot to the music. Yes, he was quite good at it, but he always had to be better than anyone else at anything. That was Kevin all over.

But this time, it just did not work out in the way he wanted. He went off at speed, crashed into some boys while he was spinning around, and went crashing into the edge of the rink's safety bumpers. He did a somersault over the railing and landed on his arm, breaking it. We all had to go back home.

Mum took Kevin to hospital to get it seen to. He came back with a plaster cast on it. In the meantime, I stayed at home with Dad, and Dad asked me what had happened at the rink that day.

I told Dad just what had happened and how Kevin had been showing off in front of the girls for a long time before he went too fast and crashed into some boys. For the next six weeks, I took the opportunity to take the mick out of Kevin quietly, just to get my own back after the London trip. After that, he never took the mick out of me again.

A few days later, we went out to play and see Babs and Nits. Kevin was feeling very sorry for himself, but he didn't get any sympathy from Babs or Nits. Their mum told Kevin how stupid he had been and how it doesn't pay to show off, does it?

Kevin just had to agree with it. He didn't show off for a long time after that. For months, Kevin started to take other people's feelings into consideration. It was great to have a normal brother who was no longer so big-headed and who didn't have to be right all the time.

Two months after the plaster cast was to come off, we were going camping with the Cubs, and by then, Kevin should be over his broken arm and okay to go. We had been looking forward to the camping trip for quite a long time, and as the time was getting closer, we were getting very excited.

Mum and Dad told us both when we went camping not to do anything stupid, like climbing trees and falling back down to earth, because that will hurt a lot more than when Kevin broke his arm. We both promised that we would do as we were told by our Scout leader.

Also, it was around that time in my life that I realised I had something going on in my head. I was finding it very hard to read books and music when I was playing my euphonium.

I just could not work out why Kevin and the kids at school could read, and I found it so hard to read and write.

But in those days, dyslexia was not recognised as a problem. You would just be labelled as a dunce and have the mick taken out of you at school and anywhere else where you were expected to read. Back then, if you couldn't read, you were classed as thick or a dummy, so I just put up with all the bullying from school and said to myself that one day, I would be better than them.

Chapter 8
Camping with the S.A. Cubs

In the summer of 1961, Kevin and I were going on a camping trip to Redcar with the Darlington S.A. Cubs. We had been looking forward to the trip for months but didn't have any proper sleeping bags. So, Mum made us some out of one sheet and two blankets folded over in half, pinned together with dress pins, and then rolled up with pieces of string to hold them together.

We packed our rucksacks the night before, ready for the first thing in the morning. It was our first trip away from home, and we were so excited that night we didn't sleep much. We talked very quietly for about four hours before eventually drifting off.

The next morning, we were both up with the larks at the crack of dawn. We had a big breakfast and went to the Salvation Army hall to be picked up for the camping trip. The bus arrived, and we all crammed our gear into the boot before setting off on our new adventure, camping out under the stars for the first time.

On the road, we all practiced singing the camp songs. When we arrived at Redcar, we went to a large wooden hut, which was empty except for a room at the other end for the leader of the pack. We all found a spot and unrolled our sleeping bags—or whatever we had—to sleep in.

The bus stopped at a farm gate, and just over the hill, we could see the tops of trees. We were told we would be setting up camp in the heart of the woods. As we entered the woods, the light changed to a very dull glow, and the strange sounds of the forest became apparent. We could hear the birds in the treetops and the rustling of animals in the undergrowth.

We arrived at a clearing by the river, where we set up camp. Afterward, we went into the woods looking for firewood, then off to explore our new surroundings. That night, we had our first meal cooked on the campfire. We sang camp songs around the fire until about nine, then settled down for the night.

The next day, we went down to the beach and played games—Cowboys and Indians in the sand dunes, or made sandcastles. We spent a couple of hours in the dunes before heading back to the hut for dinner. We had a barbecue and another sing-song in the hut.

The following day, we went to Richmond Castle. We had a whale of a time exploring the castle from top to bottom, including the deepest dungeons. It was spooky in the dungeons, and the winding stairs to the top of the castle were dark in places, adding to the eerie atmosphere.

The castle had steep steps, and the rooms were massive, damp, and echoing. In the dungeons, there were still chains on the walls where, in the old days, thieves were chained as punishment. I couldn't imagine living in those times.

We all had a great day and were very tired when we got back to the hut. After supper, we went to bed early, as we were off on a field trip the next day. It didn't take long to fall asleep, but the sounds of the night woke us up after we had our meal around the campfire.

We had left a lot of sausages in the frying pan, which we'd placed on a small box just to the right of the fire. As darkness fell, the nighttime creatures began to stir. We couldn't sleep for long due to the strange noises coming from the forest. We lay on our stomachs, peering out of the tent flaps with the light turned down very low, whispering to each other.

We heard rustling in the undergrowth, and it slowly got closer and closer. Soon, we could see two eyes between the trees, followed by two more, lower down. As they came closer, we realised they belonged to a badger and its cubs—three cubs and the mum and dad badger. They approached the camp cautiously, sniffing the air. When they reached the frying pan, the male badger sniffed it briefly, then gently took one sausage and tasted it. He made a low grunting noise, and the mother came over to take another sausage and carry it to the cubs.

Once all the sausages were gone, the badgers disappeared back into the undergrowth to find food elsewhere.

We had another activity day where there were all sorts of things to do—rope-climbing nets, rope bridges, and the ultimate rope ladder that went high up into the trees, leading to the biggest treehouse. We just had to try that out.

When I reached the bottom of the ladder, Kevin didn't want to climb up. I was a bit more adventurous, so I went up on my own. The treehouse was about halfway up the tree and was attached to another tree next to it. When I reached the top, I was given a Mars bar and told to have a breather before looking around the treehouse.

After a minute or two, I explored the treehouse. It was much bigger than it looked from the ground and had four rooms and a small balcony. There were seats in the rooms so you could watch the wildlife. It was an exhilarating experience, and I stayed up there for a long time, enjoying the view.

When it was time to go down, the rope ladder seemed much scarier than when I went up. It felt a lot higher, and I was worried I might lose my footing and fall all the way down. But, of course, I made it safely back to the ground, and that's an experience I'll never forget.

The only thing that bothered us about the camping trip was our sleeping bags—they weren't like the ones the other cubs had. We had to make do with two blankets and a sheet, folded in half and pinned together with big dress pins. But that's all Mum and Dad could afford at the time. Kevin and I didn't let it bother us; we made do, and we still enjoyed ourselves, even though some of the other cubs took the mickey out of us. We rose above it, though, because we were there to have fun.

Watching the badgers and their cubs was the best adventure of our lives.

The day at Richmond Castle was great too. We climbed to the top of the castle turrets and looked down at the people coming through the gates. From up there, they looked like ants walking below. The dungeons were spooky as we imagined the prisoners being shackled to the walls.

The view from the top was spectacular. We could see for miles across the town and over the fields. In the distance, beyond the fields, were other villages, and the cars on the roads looked like little Matchbox toy cars and buses. We stayed at the top of the castle for quite a while before heading back down.

The winding staircase down seemed much darker than when we went up, probably because we had just come out of the brilliant sunlight into the gloom.

When we all got back on the bus, we headed home.

When we got back, we told Mum, Dad, Hazel, and Joy all about our adventure—watching the badgers and their cubs taking the sausages, the treehouse, and all the other things we'd done on the camping trip. What a wonderful time we had!

The next year, Kevin and I's lives would change for good. Dad had just retired from the railways and was looking for something to keep him busy. All his life, he'd always been active, either working or with the Salvation Army.

Six months later, Dad found a new job—but it wasn't in Darlington. It was down south, in Eastbourne. Mum and Dad sat us boys down one day and explained everything in detail.

Mum was born in Eastbourne, and Dad was born in London. Dad had promised Mum a long time ago, when they first got together, that they would go back to Eastbourne one day, and that day was coming soon.

Mum told us that, in the summer holidays, we would be moving to Eastbourne to live in four weeks' time. We had time to say our goodbyes to all our friends. We were both sad and happy at the same time.

Kevin and I went into our bedroom to think it all over. We slept on it, and the next day we were both excited. We told Mum and Dad that we were looking forward to moving to the seaside soon.

Chapter 9

The Farewell from Darlington

I was now 8 years old, and Kevin was 9½. Mum and Dad asked us both what we thought about moving to live by the seaside for good. Mum then said, "Go and think about it and give us an answer at tea time." We both went off and thought about it very carefully for some time. We went up to the top of the garden, the place we loved so much. We stayed there all afternoon, talking about all the things we could do on the beach and up on the South Downs.

We also talked about all the things we would miss, like the friends we had made, especially the Alley kids, as we were all known. It was probably the hardest decision we had ever had to make.

We went in for our tea, and after a while, Mum asked, "What do you both think about moving to the seaside then, boys?"

We both said, after a short pause, "Yes, we would love to, but where would we live? And would we have a big garden to play in?" Mum said, "Not that Dad has just retired and can't deal with a big garden."

We were moving because Dad had gotten a caretaker's job at a church in Eastbourne, and we were going to live in the church flat. But there was a big veranda where we could play, and several parks nearby the church.

Mum then said, "We'll have to start packing soon. We leave next month." For the next four weeks, we talked about nothing else. We had to pack everything in the house, garden shed, and attic — and that was quite a lot of stuff. We helped Dad empty the attic too. Then, Dad and all of us had one last huge bonfire in the back garden to get rid of all the things we didn't want or that were broken. It was the biggest bonfire we had ever seen in our old back garden. By now, the big day was just two days away.

On Saturday, we went out to say goodbye to all our friends in the back alleys. It was a very sad time, and yet a very exciting time. We didn't know quite how to feel — the sadness of moving and leaving all our friends behind, the excitement of going to the seaside — it was too much for both of us. We took a slow walk back home that day, both of us with tears in our eyes, but we stopped by the time we got home.

On the last Sunday, we went to the Salvation Army in Darlington for the last time to say goodbye to all our friends there. That Sunday, there was a surprise farewell for us. The meeting finished early, and there was a presentation to Mum and Dad for all the hard work they had put in over the last 50 years. For once, Mum and Dad were totally gobsmacked.

When we went back home that day, our hearts were heavy with sorrow, saddened to be leaving for good, but at the same time, looking forward to living by the seaside.

The big day had come. The removal Lorries arrived, and the men started loading up. Kevin and I went to say our last goodbye to Ruby, who ran the sweet shop on the corner of the road. When we got to the shop, Ruby gave us both a huge bag of sweets for the long journey to our "new home" and told us both to take good care of each other and good luck. "We'll miss you all," she said.

We went back to the only home we knew. It was time to leave Park Crescent for the last time. We both took one last look at the garden, then climbed into the back of Mum's car. Mum had an Austin A40, or "Little Fe-Fe," as Mum called it because of the number plate FEF 783.

And off we went on the long journey to Eastbourne, out of Darlington and into the countryside, and then onto the motorway heading south.

We had been on the road for nearly three hours when we stopped at a motorway service station for the first time. We had some lunch and a loo stop, as Dad called it. The car park seemed to go on forever, and the café was big, but the food was great.

Kevin and I were both called "Sir" by the waitress. We felt very important. After finishing our meal, we got back in the car and hit the road again. Dad said, "The next time we stop, we'll be just outside of London, where we had our holiday last year. We'll be quite close to Eastbourne by then."

We arrived at another motorway café just 30 miles outside of London. We had our tea there, then only had 100 miles to go.

Dad said, "The next stop will be Eastbourne, but it will be dark by then, and we will be travelling through the countryside."

When we got back in the car for the last leg of the journey, Mum said, "If you want to have a bit of a kip, boys, we'll wake you up just before we get to Eastbourne."

Kevin and I did have a sleep in the back of the car during the last part of the journey, as we passed through the pitch-black countryside. When we were about 10 miles from Eastbourne, Dad woke us up. "We're nearly there, boys," he said. "Only about 10 miles to go before we can see the lights of Eastbourne."

The road seemed to go on for hours, but then Mum said, "Soon, boys, you'll see the streetlights of Eastbourne. First the glow, and then the lights suddenly."

Mum wasn't kidding when she said we'd see the lights suddenly. We carried on down the road, and soon we saw the glow of the Eastbourne streetlights. Mum said, "Keep watching, boys, and don't take your eyes off the road ahead, and you'll see the lights coming at you suddenly." And boy, she wasn't kidding.

We saw the road disappear down, and the Eastbourne lights suddenly appeared to come straight towards us. For a moment, we thought the car was going to crash straight into the lights, but the road went down into Eastbourne.

We both said, "WOW!" as we slowed down to 30 mph for the drive into Eastbourne town and onto the hotel on the seafront for the night.

We settled down in the hotel room and looked out of the window. We could see the moonlight gleaming on the waves as they splashed onto the beach. Then, we went straight off to sleep, well and truly knackered after the long journey down to Eastbourne.

The next day, we got up very early after a good night's sleep. We could hear the waves breaking on the shore. We went down for breakfast and had a good old English breakfast with extra toast.

Then we went to see our new home on Wish Road. Dad was to be the new caretaker of the church. Little did I know then, these were to be the best days of my life.

As we went through the big wrought-iron gates, we had to go up a metal fire escape to the first landing. On the left was a wooden door that led onto the veranda, and on the right were the French doors that opened into the flat.

The flat was very long and had three bedrooms, a bathroom, a kitchen, a living room, a large front room, and a corridor that ran the full length of the flat. There were stairs at the other end that went down into the church, and two sets of stairs that went up to the bedrooms and bathroom.

We were both excited and unhappy to have just moved away from all our friends in Darlington, but we soon got over it when the next day came.

Chapter 10
Looking Around Eastbourne The 1st Time

The next day, most of the unpacking had been done. Mum said to us, "Do you want to go for a ride on your bikes, boys?" We said yes, and off we went to see the seafront for the first time.

We went up the road and onto the seafront. Once we were there, we took note of the landmark and walked along the bottom promenade, all the way down to the foot of the South Downs. We found a hidden café at a place called Hollywell. We went in and ordered a coffee, something we weren't allowed to drink at home. Mum had always said it would keep us awake at night if we drank too much of it, but we wanted to try it anyway. It was very nice.

We sat in the sun at a table with our sandwiches and baskets Mum had packed for us. It wasn't long before we noticed something moving in the undergrowth. We sat very still so as not to frighten whatever it was. We waited, and then, to our surprise, a small head appeared from under the bushes just in front of us. We were looking at a weasel. It came closer, and we gave it some of our food. At first, it was a bit timid, but we managed to gain its trust during the time it stayed with us.

We went back home and told Mum and Dad where we had been. Mum said, "I'd forgotten that café was still there." We never did tell Mum and Dad that we both had coffee at the café that day.

The next day was Sunday. We always went to the Salvation Army meetings all day, and Dad said that a Sunday roast was a tradition for our family.

The next day was Monday, and it was back to school. Kevin and I didn't look forward to school because there was a boy who always stole our sweets. One day, I went to my friend Vernon's house. Vernon told his mum all about the boy at school who stole our sweets. Vernon's mum said, "That's easy to stop." She went to the food cupboard, took out a very small bar of chocolate, and said, "Go to the shop and get two small bars of chocolate. They must be the same size as this one."

We looked puzzled at the time, but Vernon's mum urged us to go ahead and see what would happen. So off we went to the shop, bought the chocolate, and took it back to Vernon's mum. She said, "Now, slide the chocolate out of the wrappers, but don't tear the wrappers." We did this very carefully and handed the two bars of chocolate to her. She then said, "You can have that yourself, Brian, just keep the wrappers."

Then, Vernon's mum very carefully slid the two bars of chocolate into the wrappers of the ones we had just bought. She explained, "Tomorrow, when the boy comes to steal your sweets, give him this instead. Just before he goes into the classroom, watch and see how embarrassed he becomes after about half an hour. This is laxative chocolate. It means that when he eats it, he'll have to go to the loo or he'll do it in his pants."

We both agreed that he'd never steal sweets again after that.

The next day, we met up on our way to school to make our plans. As we went through the school gates, we saw the boy on the other side of the playground stealing sweets from a group of kids. We stayed out of his way until we were asked to line up. Just then, the boy came over to us, and we gave him the laxative chocolate. Sure enough, he stuffed it all in his mouth just before he went into the classroom.

Vernon and I always sat two desks behind the boy. While the teacher was doing the register, the boy started to fidget in his seat. He put up his hand and asked if he could go to the loo. The teacher said, "No, you've just come into the classroom. You should have gone before you came in."

The boy kept fidgeting, and he just couldn't hold it any longer. He let out the biggest fart the class had ever heard, and the smell was overwhelming. The whole class turned to look, and we saw him with runny poo all down his legs, on his seat, and on the floor. He was in a huge mess, and all the teacher could say was, "See, you've been eating too many sweets again, Jamey. Serves you right. Now go to the headmaster's office," knowing he would have to wait a while for the door to be answered.

The whole class teased him for the rest of our school days, and the boy never bullied anyone again. I wonder why.

Just over two years later, Vernon went to France during the school holidays with his cousins on a day trip. Sadly, he was run over by a hit-and-run driver on a crossing and died three weeks later in a French hospital. I will always miss him. We had some great times together, racing on our homemade go-carts.

The years seemed to fly by, and soon it was my last few years at school. By then, I was 10 years old, and I still didn't like school much. I often had Ready Brek for breakfast. One day, I opened a new packet and saw an offer on the back. By saving tokens, we could get a Ready Brek farm layout. I loved being around animals more than anything else, and seemed much happier with them than with people. Mum said, "We'll save up for it then. You might have enough tokens by Christmas."

That was in January, and Christmas seemed a long way off. So, we saved the tokens all year, and my birthday came and went in June. As Christmas drew closer, I asked Mum if I would have enough tokens for the farm by Christmas. She told me I still had a bit to go but might have enough by my birthday next year, when I would turn 11.

On Bonfire Night, we always had fireworks in the back garden. Dad took control of the bonfire and fireworks at the top of the garden, and we all stood at the bottom of the garden, under the kitchen window, watching them go off. When the fireworks were over, we had baked potatoes that had been cooked in the bonfire. Afterward, Dad doused the flames with buckets of water before bedtime. Kevin and I would often look out of the bedroom window to see what shapes we could spot in the embers of the fire.

The next day was a Sunday, and it was going to be a bit different because there would be a special presentation for Brigadier Denials and his wife. They were retiring from their missionary work. They had spent their whole lives caring for unfortunate children across the world, many suffering from malnutrition and disease. On that Sunday, the young people's band was going to perform for them. I and Kevin had to sit on the platform in the band. Brigadier Denials' hobby was breeding budgies, and they had brought one in a cage with them. During the service, the bird chirped while we sang and went quiet during prayer.

The next day was back to school. Kevin and I walked together every day, and I always met up with my friend Owen. But this day felt different because it was to be our last term at school. We said we were going to leave school with a bang, but it was only a saying. We didn't mean it literally. When we got to the school gates, I had only one thing on my mind: working on a farm.

Chapter 11

The New School

As usual, the school bullies were waiting for us, and I was fed up with them after five years of constant bullying. Owen and I both muttered, "Here we go again," as we walked through the gate.

I said, "Not this time."

Most mornings, the bullies would pin us up against the wall, but this time something was different. I suddenly got a surge of adrenaline. Without thinking, I picked up the biggest bully with one hand and held him above my head. With my other hand, I grabbed the bully's belt buckle, lifting his whole body above me. Then, I knelt on one knee and let the bully drop, stomach first, onto my knee, winding him.

"Okay, who's next?" I asked.

With that, the bullies kept well out of our way for the rest of the term. There were no further problems.

In the last four weeks of the term, we had a double Science lesson. The Science teacher wanted to try out a new experiment. He explained the process in detail, telling us there were six stages, with the fourth stage being the most crucial. We had to warm up the experiment very, very slowly over the afternoon break using a very low Bunsen burner.

We all followed the instructions carefully up to the third stage. The fourth stage came at break time, but as we were leaving the classroom, the teacher went out first, and we all followed. However, as we were heading out, Owen turned the gas up on two of the experiments and added the leftovers to the two experiments belonging to the bullies, hoping to get them into trouble. The teacher didn't seem to notice as he slammed the door shut.

Owen and I moved to the other side of the playground, far from the Science lab. As we sat down, Owen told me what he had done. I said, "What would you do if the lab blew up?"

Owen, with great confidence, replied, "Of course it won't. (Famous last words.)"

We kept a close eye on the lab. About half an hour into the lunch break, we saw little bits of grey and blue smoke coming from the lab's windows.

"Look at the lab!" I said.

Owen replied, "I know. I said I wanted to go out of school with a big bang, but this is not what I flipping meant."

I said, "You've done it now."

"You don't think it will explode, do you?" Owen asked.

"I flipping hope not."

Too late—it happened.

There was a huge explosion, followed by rockets and all sorts of things going off at the back of the lab. We had just blown up the school's fireworks for the November 5th display.

The other kids in the playground thought it was great when the fireworks went off, but the teacher on duty panicked. He shouted for everyone to move to the other side of the playground. We didn't mind. There was a better view from that side. It was great.

Owen and I decided not to own up to it, as we knew we'd be expelled, and we didn't see the point. No one got hurt, apart from the surprise fireworks going off earlier than planned. We both stayed quiet. We were leaving school in three weeks anyway, and then it would be on to work. I was looking forward to it.

After school ended, I had some time to think about what I wanted to do with the rest of my life. All I really wanted to do was work on a farm with animals, as I still felt I could communicate with them better than with people. Even though I'd been attacked by that sheepdog years ago, I was now over it, though I was still cautious about trusting animals. The attack had made me more thoughtful before trusting any animal, but I wasn't scared of them.

I was often worried about where I was headed in life. Sometimes it weighed on my mind, and I couldn't get it out of my head that my real parents had given me up for adoption. I tried to put it out of my mind and move on, but it kept coming back from time to time.

When I was younger, I would often go out of Darlington into the countryside to see the farm animals in the fields. I'd stand by the gate for hours. One day, I was standing there when the farmer came up to me and said, "I've seen you many times standing here. What are you up to, boy?"

I told the farmer that I wanted to work on a farm when I was older. He said it was a good life working with animals and that he did it because he felt he could relate to the animals better than he could with his wife. Animals seemed better than humans in many ways, he said.

I told the farmer that I had been adopted and that I felt the same way as he did—that I thought I was the only one in the world who felt that way. But the farmer said, "You're not alone in feeling that way. All the farmers in the world feel the same. That's why they're farmers. They have a great respect for God's creatures."

"One day, would you like to come and see what farming is really about?" the farmer asked.

I said, "Yes, please," and went home to tell Mum and Dad all about it. Two or three weeks later, I went back to the farm. The farmer gave me a tour and showed me what farming life was truly like. It was wonderful to see how well the animals were looked after.

I fed the pigs, baby cows, and lambs, and I got to see the farm machinery. The farmer explained how the combine harvester cut the corn in the summer and how the bales of hay were made for winter bedding.

One day, the bull was in the field where the cows had been a couple of days before. I wondered where the cows had gone. Just then, the farmer came down the road in one of the tractors and saw me at the gate. When he stopped, I asked him where the cows had gone.

He replied, "The cows have been moved to another field on the other side of the farm. The bull is in this field now, ready for some new cows I'm getting from the market next week. The bull won't be on his own for long. We can't breed the same cows every year. They need a rest for two years. Do you understand that?"

I said I could see the logic in what he was saying. The farmer then told me to jump up into the tractor and help feed the chickens and ducks. So, I hopped up into the cab of the tractor, and we took a bumpy ride to the farm.

I spent the morning feeding the chickens and ducks and their chicks and ducklings. It was wonderful to feed the babies from my hand. I had a great time.

On the farm, I made up my mind: when I was older, I wanted to work on a farm for the rest of my life.

As I rode home that day on my bike, I thought about what a wonderful life it would be if I could become a farmer.

About a mile from home, there was a railway bridge where I stopped for a short rest. I watched the trains going by on the line above and remembered when Kevin and I were little. We would stand on the railway bridge at Darlington Station before heading back home.

Chapter 12
My 1st Job.

I was 15 years old, and life was going to be so much harder now in the real world.

I went to the Dole office just at the end of the road from the church where I lived. It was the first time I had been in the Dole office. I had passed it many times as a child coming back from school, but this time, I had to go in with the real men looking for work. When I went in, the office was nearly empty for a change. Back then, there were more jobs than there were people to fill them, so I went to the desk and spoke to a man who was there to help you get a job.

I explained what sort of job I was looking for – farm work. The man looked on his list to see what was available. There was a job coming up for a farm labourer, but it wasn't to start for another 12 months. In the meantime, there was a job in a warehouse at a local food store. I said I would take the job, and off I went for my first interview.

In those days, jobs were ten a penny, and it wasn't long before I was set to start my new job. The next Monday was my first day of working for a living and earning a wage.

I went back home and told my mum and dad. Dad said, "The way to get on in your working life is simple: just keep your nose clean. And if you see someone else stealing something from work, quietly report it, but be discreet. Don't let the person know you've done it. Good luck for Monday, and well done."

Mum said, "Now that you'll be earning a wage, the first wage is mine to keep. But from the next one, you'll have to pay us some housekeeping money or rent of £1.00 a week." Back then, £1.00 was a lot of money, as the wage I was going to be getting was £5.10s 6d a week.

I was okay with that. I could open a bank account for the first time, as well as the Post Office account I already had. Not that there was much in it, but it was a start. After all, from small acorns, trees will grow.

Monday came, and I went off to work. I got there early, as instructed by my new boss. I arrived 35 minutes early, and my new boss was already there, waiting. The shop wasn't open yet, but he just wanted to show me around the store and explain what I would be doing on a day-to-day basis. By the time my new boss had finished telling me about the job, I thought, "Wow, this is going to be some challenge."

My boss told me not to try and keep up with the rest of the workers straight away, as they wouldn't expect me to on my first day. But by the time I had been there for four months, I should be able to keep up with the rest of them.

In those days, when the Lorries came in with their deliveries, all the stock came down the rollers of the lorry, down the shoot onto another set of rollers, and into the warehouse. We then had to stack it onto pallets for storage inside the warehouse. It was very hard work, but I soon got the hang of where everything went and how it all worked. After two months, I was as quick as the rest of the workforce.

The pallets were not as they are now. They had two wheels at the back and a ball in the middle at the front to put the pulley wheels into. They weren't very safe when you took a corner, but I got used to them before too many mishaps occurred.

Kevin was also working in the food shop. He was filling shelves all day and going on the till. He was very happy in his job and had had it since he left school.

I had been in my job for eight months, and my muscles were quite big, which was just as well, as I would need them when I started the farm job I really wanted to do.

Soon, a letter arrived for me saying that the farm job was mine if I still wanted it. I wrote back to confirm it and received the starting date. I told my boss, and a month later, I left the food store job behind.

I arranged to go to the farm to meet the farmer a week later. When I arrived, I went up to the house and knocked on the door. I waited for a couple of minutes, and the farmer's wife answered the door and asked what I wanted.

I said that I had an appointment with the farmer about a job. The farmer's wife told me I'd better come in and wait, as the farmer was sorting out a cow that was having trouble calving.

"Would you like a cup of tea while you wait?" she asked.

I said, "Yes, please." About an hour and a half later, the farmer came back, saw me sitting and having my second cup of tea, and said, "Sorry to keep you waiting, but that's the way it is working with animals and farm life."

The farmer had a cup of tea, then showed me around the farm. There was so much for me to remember, all the different things that were expected of me. I told him I was sure I would get the hang of it. He said I would, in time, and that I was going to make some mistakes at first.

"So long as they're not big ones, don't worry," he said. "You'll be mucking out to start with after milking time, and generally helping all over the farm."

I told the farmer that I couldn't start for two weeks, as I was finishing up my notice at the shop job while I was waiting for a farm job to come up.

The farmer said, "That's okay, you can start in two weeks' time then. But you must be here and ready to start work by 3:15 a.m. every day, seven days a week. Is that okay with you?"

I said, "Yes," and the tour around the farm was over. The farmer said, "See you in two weeks' time then, and don't be late."

I told him I would be on time and not to worry. We shook hands, and I made my way back home.

On the way back, I thought that this would mean I wouldn't be able to go to the Salvation Army on Sundays, but I wasn't that bothered about that. It was a small price to pay, as I would finally be doing the one thing I'd always wanted to do – work with animals on a farm.

Chapter 13
Starting On The Farm

Soon, I would have to get my dream job, the one I had always wanted since I was a young boy: to work on a farm with animals and not much else. It wasn't long before that dream became a reality, and I started working on a farm on the outskirts of Eastbourne, just past the village of Langney.

The first day working on the farm was the best day of my life. I arrived early and went to the big house—that's what they called the farmhouse. The farmer and I went to the milking sheds, and he showed me how to chain the cows up when they came in to be milked. He told me never to stand behind the cows, as they might kick out, and that could really hurt.

Soon after, the cows came in for milking. It was a bit scary at first, but I soon got used to it. The cows were more scared of us than we were of them. I had to clean the cows' teats for the milking machine to get the milk after milking time.

We all went up to the big house for a cooked breakfast, and after that, I went back to the milking sheds to scrub out the stalls and get them ready for the afternoon milking. By the time I had finished, it was time to feed the calves. I was taught how to get the calves to drink from a bucket using an artificial teat and then to drink on their own.

It was great. I really felt like I belonged, working on the farm with the animals. It was as if I was born to do this kind of work. Even though the work was hard and tiring at times, I was happy. After working on the farm for two years, I became very strong, both mentally and physically.

I still went to the army when I could on Sundays, and Kevin was getting a bit jealous of the muscles I had built up from working so hard on the farm. The girls from the singing company always seemed to be around me more than him. Even though Kevin's heart and mind were always on a girl from the singing company back in Darlington, a curly-haired girl named Marjory, he was very fond of her. They wrote to each other all the time and sometimes rang each other on weekends, even though they lived 400 miles apart.

I had been working on the farm for just over two and a half years, and harvest time was approaching. It was a very busy time of year, what with the lambing calves being born and the usual things—milking, etc. By then, I was in my element, working on the farm. I got on very well with the farmer and his family, especially the farmer's niece, J. She was 17 years old, the same age as me. We had good fun together as well as working well together.

One day, J and I were having lunch in the barn after filling it up with bales of hay from that year's harvest. The hay was still warm from the sun. J asked me, "Shall we go up to the top of the stack?" I said, "Yes, why not?" We climbed to the very top. We were about five feet from the roof, and boy, was it hot up there!

It wasn't long before we were both sweating buckets. We stripped off all our clothes and lay in the hay together. J had a gorgeous figure, and it wasn't long before the inevitable happened. We made love. After the first time, we did it quite often that year until J went to college.

Later that year, the farmer asked me to keep an eye on a bonfire near the duck shed, which was falling apart, just until I had to go and get the cows in for milking. It was a calm day, hardly any wind, just a light breeze. I sat down to have my dinner, and by the time I was ready to get the cows in for milking, the bonfire was nearly out. There were just red embers glowing.

So, I went over the road to get the cows from the three fields beyond the farm, over the hill, and into the third field. I called to the cows, as we always did, "Come on then," and they would come to you, and that's how you got the cows in.

As I was coming back to the farm with the cows, over the second field and up the hill, I saw smoke coming from the direction of the farm. I thought to myself, "Don't tell me the duck shed has caught fire."

I remembered what I had said to the farmer about the bonfire being too close to the duck shed, but the farmer had told me, "What do you know about bonfires? Just keep an eye on it while you're on dinner." As I got closer to the farm, my worst fears were confirmed—it was the duck shed that had caught fire, and the fire brigade was there with two fire engines putting it out.

I took the cows to the milking yard and waited until it was their turn to be milked. Then, I went to see what was left of the duck shed. Not much. It had burned to the ground. The farmer was furious and was blaming me for it. He told me to go and do the milking and then come to see him at the big house when I had cleaned out the milking sheds.

After finishing with the milking and mucking out, I went to the big house. The farmer gave me the biggest roasting of my life. He told me I was finished with farming anywhere in the country. He handed me my wages up to the day before the fire and told me I had time to get my things out of my locker in the barn and get off his property.

I argued with him, saying it wasn't my fault, and that I had warned him that the bonfire was too close to the duck shed. The farmer denied any knowledge of what I had said and just repeated, "Get your things and get off my land," with a very angry look on his face.

So, I went to pick up my things and had a quick last look at the farm where I had been so happy for nearly three years. I got back on my pushbike and went down the lane. As I rode back home, I just couldn't hold back my tears. I stopped about three miles down the road and just let it all out. I sobbed my heart out, and after a while, I pulled myself together and made my way home.

All I could think about was what I was going to tell Mum and Dad when I got back from work early. When I got home, they were waiting for me. They already knew all about it. I explained that I hadn't started the fire, but they just wouldn't believe me.

I was sent to see a shrink and then to court, where I was given two years' probation, during which I had to see a probation officer every week. All of this for something I knew I hadn't done.

Later, I found out that the fire at the farm had been set on purpose so the farmer could cash in on the insurance. The farmer was going to retire from farming and was trying to get as much money as he could for a nice, comfortable retirement.

It didn't matter that I had been labelled as some kind of evil-minded person with an unbalanced mind, which couldn't have been further from the truth.

But that was it. My idea of working on a farm for the rest of my life was well and truly over, and somehow, I had to get my head around it all and move on with my life.

I had enjoyed working on the farm, but it had only been for 5 and a half years. The farmer ended my job and dashed my hopes and dreams of becoming a farmer. There are some evil people in this world, as I had just found out the hard way.

I had put so much trust and belief into the farmer, thinking he was as honest as I was, but now I knew I couldn't trust anyone again.

I had to go on the dole for about six months or so until I could get my head around it all. I was so angry about the farmer and the way I had been treated over the fire, and how I had been wrongly blamed for it. I now had the label of arsonist, but for now, I just had to live with it and try to move on with my life, forgetting all about becoming a farmer.

I concentrated on finding a new job over the next six months. It wasn't long before a job came up.

Chapter 14

My Rebelling Teenage Years

Mum told me that she had found a job for me working with my Uncle Fred on a building site in a new posh area of Eastbourne. The houses we were building cost over £350,000 each.

I went to see Uncle Fred and got started straight away, on a site in the posh area of Eastbourne. On the site, there was an old caravan that served as the office and canteen. There, I met the rest of the workforce, had a cup of tea, and then went on to the site. The house that was being built was about halfway to completion—the first floor was almost finished.

My job was to unload the deliveries of bricks and cement when they arrived and to keep the bricklayers supplied with mortar and bricks. I was already quite strong from working on the farm, and this job was only going to make me even stronger.

It didn't take long for me to get used to my new job. I was a bit naive—I hadn't had much experience of what the outside world was really like or what some people could be like.

It wasn't long before I was going to find out. Five months after I started, one of the bricklayers, named John, started to take a bit more interest in me. One summer's day, I had been working all morning with my shirt off, just like a lot of the men on the site did.

At lunchtime, I sat on a stack of cement bags, and John came and sat beside me. He started talking to me, saying that I was a good worker, that I worked hard, and that no job on the site seemed too much for me. He even commented on how strong my muscles looked. At the time, I just took it as a compliment.

A few weeks later, the first floor was completed, and the roof framework was on. The floorboards had just arrived, and it was just John and me on the site, getting the floorboards up inside the shell of the building. It was a very hot day in the middle of summer, and we both had our shirts off, as always. There was nothing unusual about that day, apart from the searing heat.

The boards were stacked up on one side of a large room inside the building. When we stopped for dinner, we decided, as it was so hot, to have it inside, sitting on the floorboards. It was like an oven that day. Both John's and my feet were throbbing from the intense heat. I asked John if he minded if I took my boots off for a bit to let my feet cool down. He said he was just about to ask me the same thing, so we both took off our boots to cool down while we ate. It was bliss to be in the shade for a while.

But after dinner, when I was putting my boots back on, John started to touch me—first on my back and shoulders. I stood up and asked him what he thought he was doing. He said, "I'm gay, and I fancy you. Will you come back home with me after work?" I pushed him off, in disgust, and told him to get lost, but with words a lot stronger than that.

Just after dinner, my Uncle Fred came back on site and saw that the floorboards had arrived and had been put up inside the building. Uncle Fred said, "Well done," to both John and me and went into the office. John was still inside the building, so I went and had a word with my uncle, telling him all about what had happened during dinner.

Uncle Fred just said that he knew all about John and that he was gay. He told me he wasn't going to do anything about it because John was a fast worker.

So, for the next seven months, I avoided John until the job was finished. When the building was completed, all the bricklayers moved on to a new site, and the rest of us lads were left behind to clean up the site so the new owners could move in. Five weeks later, while I was working those final weeks, I got talking to some of the other lads about John. I was told I wasn't the only one John had tried it on with.

The lads said to me, "Welcome to the real world. Don't worry about it. John will try it again somewhere else."

By then, I was 17 and a half years old, and all I wanted to do was leave home and get a place of my own. I had saved up some money from working and was looking forward to it—the thought of an unknown life to come, doing what I wanted when I wanted to, without being constantly told what I could and couldn't do by my foster parents.

By now, I had been rebelling against my foster parents for the last 7 or 8 years. I just couldn't get my head around the fact that my biological parents didn't want to know me or Kevin, even though Kevin wasn't bothered about it. I was.

I left my job with Uncle Fred and got all my wages that I was owed in cash—£284.2/6d—and went back home, the day before my 18th birthday.

When I got back home that day, Mum and Dad were waiting for me and greeted me with these words: "You'd better give us all the £284.2/6d for your board and lodging for the next few weeks."

For the first time, I stood up to Mum and Dad and said, in a very firm voice, "No."

Dad came over to take the money off me, but I pushed him over the arm of the sofa. Mum said, "You're 18 tomorrow. You can get out."

I said, "That's fine by me," and went into my bedroom to pack up my things. Mum and Dad came to my room and told me I could stay for breakfast the next day, but that tonight would be my last night, and then I was on my own. I said, "That suits me just fine."

The next day came, and after breakfast, I left home for good. I wasn't going to look back.

Chapter 15
Leaving Home

I had been working for my Uncle Fred for some time, but things weren't going well at home. I was still rebelling from being adopted 15 years earlier. I just couldn't shake the feeling that the world was always against me, but I never talked about it. I kept it all to myself. Anyway, my 18th birthday was approaching, and I started thinking about getting a place of my own. Little did I know how close I was to making that a reality in just a few weeks.

I had to quit my job with my uncle because there was a man working there who was a creep and always after the young lads, me included. So, I left the day before my 18th birthday. I went to the site to collect the wages I was owed, and on my way back home, I stopped to count it.

I had just received £265.10/-7d, which was a lot of money in those days, considering that my take-home pay was only about £37.2/-6d a week. When I got home that day, I had just taken off my boots when Mum said, "You'd better give me all the £265.10/-7d you got today in wages." And for the first time in my life, I stood my ground and said, "No."

My dad came over to me and tried to hit me, but I lashed out and punched him hard. He fell backward over the armchair and landed on the sofa. Mum then said, "It's your 18th birthday tomorrow. You're old enough to go your own way. You can find alternative accommodation starting tomorrow."

I stormed out of the room, went into my bedroom, and started packing.

The next day, Mum said I could have breakfast, but after that, I had to go. Dad stayed in bed until I had left. After breakfast, I grabbed my bag and suitcase and headed off to the Labour Exchange. On the way, I bumped into an old friend, Dave, who I had known from a few years before. He, too, was homeless. We decided to put our money together and find a double flat by nightfall.

We searched all over Eastbourne with no luck, so we went into a café for a coffee and a bite to eat. While we were there, we asked the owner if he knew of any flats available. He told us to try a place called Booth's Hotel. The name rang a bell, and I said, "It's the old Salvation Army Hotel." We hoped there would be room for us.

When we got there, we were in luck. The rent was only £6.7/-6d a week, and we were told we could apply for a rent rebate from the D.H.S.S. They showed us a double room. It wasn't much, but at least we had a roof over our heads. It had two single beds, a sink, two wardrobes, and a shower.

We dumped our suitcases in the middle of the floor and flopped down on the beds for a while. After that, we went to the shops to buy essentials like coffee. There was a small kitchen in our room, but we had to share a larger kitchen with others on the floor. We didn't mind, though—we had a place to call home, and beggars couldn't be choosers.

We settled in and created a kind of routine: sleeping most of the day and drinking at night. Life was great for months. We were picking up girls at night and waking up with different ones most mornings. Well, you've got to spread your wild oats while you can.

Ten months later, the money we had started with had almost run out. By then, we both had regular girlfriends, whom we had been with for about three months. We decided to go to London's Covent Garden to find work. We had just enough money for the train fare, and the girls said they would look after the flat while we were away.

When we got to London, we both found night jobs—one unloading Lorries and the other working in a café. That meant we were well sorted for free meals. We worked hard for the next six weeks, and when we could no longer carry on, we came back to Eastbourne.

We had earned enough to take a taxi home, but instead, we tried to hitch a ride. By the time we got a lift, we were three miles from Polegate, just seven miles outside Eastbourne.

When we arrived back, we spent the next few days resting. We slept for almost a week, and when we woke up, we had a doctor with us. All we wanted to do was use the loo. After that, we went out for a huge slap-up breakfast and then took a long walk along the beach. We sat on the beach for some time, and on the way back, we decided to save some of the money we had earned in London for a rainy day.

A few weeks later, Dave and Silver got married at the Eastbourne Registry Office. Dave moved out of the flat and into a place with Silver, and Tony, a friend of ours, moved in with me. He seemed alright at first. The day he moved in, he wasn't too happy with the wardrobe space, but he made do. We sat down and decided how to split things like shopping money, etc.

However, that didn't last long. A couple of months later, I realised that Tony had been dipping into the shopping money jar on a regular basis, leaving us short just before payday. He also hadn't been paying his full share of the rent. I found out when the landlord came to see me one day when Tony was out.

Mike and I had a coffee and discussed the rent problem. The rent was £11.10/-6d a week, and the arrears were £45.4/-11d. I made arrangements to pay it all back later that day, on the condition that Tony moved out by the weekend. Mike agreed. Tony was found another flat on the top floor, at a slightly reduced rate. He was thrilled and happy to move out, but what he didn't know was that the reduced rate was only for a month. After that, the rent would go up to cover the arrears from when he had been sharing with me.

A couple of months later, I found a better flat in the centre of town, just up the road from the station. It had its own kitchen, and the bathroom was just down the hall. And no Tony—peace at last! I stayed in the flat for over a year, mostly on my own.

Then I met up with Dave again, after he had split from Silver. Dave told me he was now with a woman called Les, who was pregnant with his first child. I went with Dave to meet Les, and we were invited for dinner. While we were there, Dave and Les told me about a friend of theirs called Jan, who had two girls.

A few days later, I was introduced to Jan at her home for dinner. Things went really well between us. We just seemed to hit it off straight away. After dinner, we talked for a long time, and I met the girls, Emma and Vienna, for the first time, though only for a short while.

It was getting late, so I stayed overnight in Jan's bed. In the morning, we all went downstairs for breakfast. The girls seemed a little surprised to see me still there, but they didn't seem too bothered. They just accepted it. After breakfast, I arranged to see Jan again sometime the next week. A couple of months later, I moved in with her and the girls.

I was working at a hotel at the time, and everything was great for a long while. Just over two years later, Jan got pregnant with our first child—her third, but my first. I was looking forward to the birth in February 1982.

The Christmas before the baby was born, Jan was quite ill with pre-eclampsia and had to stay in hospital for some time. She was released just in time for Christmas Eve.

Christmas came and went, and soon the time for the arrival of my first child was drawing near. I was about to become a dad for the first time.

January 1982 came with a vengeance, and Christmas was over for another year. My first child was due to be born in February of that year. On the 17th of February 1982, I called an ambulance to take Jan to the hospital. For the next three days, I paced up and down the corridors of the hospital, waiting for the baby to be born. On the third night, Jan's waters broke, and as they did, Gemma was born, weighing 9lb 5oz.

At the same time as her waters broke, one of the nurses caught Gemma as she slid off the end of the bed. We were told at the hospital that Gemma had a small heart murmur, which wasn't anything to worry about. Some babies have one, and 99.99% grow out of it in the first 3 to 5 years of life, so it was nothing at all to be concerned about. They did some more checks and gave us the all-clear.

We were both over the moon when Gemma was born. I went back home, and the next day I brought Emma and Virginia in to see the new addition to the family. They were very happy and looking forward to Gemma coming home from the hospital. Just a few days later, we took Gemma home. But on the second day back, Gemma didn't seem quite right.

So, we called the doctor out, and he called 999. We found ourselves back at the DGH, where it was discovered that Gemma didn't have a heart murmur after all. She had a hole in her heart between the two sections.

We were rushed to Great Ormond Street in London, where Gemma had a major heart operation to correct the hole. Gemma was in London for six weeks, and as she was getting stronger, we thought things were looking better. The doctors did too, but Gemma's condition worsened quickly, and she had to have another heart operation. We were once again left to play the waiting game.

Two months later, Gemma took a turn for the worse. She had to go through yet another heart operation, and after the third, sadly, Gemma died in my arms. She took one last look at me with her big blue eyes, gave a big sigh, and passed away.

Jan and I went back home to make the funeral arrangements. Then, we sat down together and cried. When we pulled ourselves together, Jan said, "Don't you think you'd better ring your mum and dad to tell them?" "Yes, I will tonight," I replied.

That night, I rang my mum and told her to sit down because I had some bad news. Mum said she too had some bad news to tell me, but she said I should go first. I then told her that my little Gemma had died that very afternoon at 3:15 p.m. Mum said how sorry she was to hear it.

I managed to ask, "What was the bad news you had to tell me?" Mum said, "Are you sitting down?" I said yes. "Well, at 3:14 p.m. that very afternoon, Dad had also passed away."

It was just too much for me to bear. I burst into tears on the stairs while still on the phone to Mum. I didn't think when I put the phone down. I went into the front room and told Jan that my dad had also died. And all Jan could say was, "Yes, so? What do you want, a medal?"

Two weeks later, we had Gemma's funeral at our local cemetery church in our hometown. At the funeral, I ripped the crucifix from my neck and threw it onto Gemma's grave. It landed on top of Gemma's coffin, the right way up, just below the plaque on the lid.

After the funeral, we went to Jan's mum's house for the wake and a bite to eat, though I didn't feel much like eating. We then went back home, but things were never the same after that. In the months that followed, Jan and I found it increasingly hard to talk to each other. Jan started to blame me for putting the hole in Gemma's heart.

I was put on antidepressants to try and help me cope, but it was all too much for me—the loss of both my dad and Gemma, all on the same day.

Just a few months later, Jan and I split up. Jan was still blaming me for Gemma's condition. She had convinced herself that I had somehow caused it. She didn't understand that I was also grieving for the loss of my dad as well as Gemma. It was all just too much for me.

Jan told me to find somewhere else to live, and I could leave all my things there until I had found a new place. So, reluctantly, I got on my motorbike to find a new home for myself.

I had been on the road for several hours, looking around friends and family, but with no luck. I went to a café for a coffee and a cigarette or two. While I was sitting there, an old friend and his girlfriend came in and saw me. They joined me and bought me a coffee. I told them everything that had happened over the past six months.

I went to live with Dave and Kim. Yes, Dave was with someone new again, in Polegate just outside Eastbourne, a village. I slapped on the sofa for the next six months. A friend of theirs, called Sue, came to stay for two weeks for a holiday but stayed longer when she found out she had been kicked out, just like me. We helped each other out for some time, and the inevitable happened—we got together and started going out.

Things started getting a bit crowded at Kim and Dave's, and Kim and Dave were arguing a lot. So, Sue and I decided to move out together. We first went to live in a pre-fab at Kings Caravan Site for three months. It was damp and due to be demolished, just a temporary measure until we could move into the Bramar Hotel Flats, just down the road from Eastbourne Pier. Everything was in one room, but it was cosy.

We stayed in a lot, but we didn't mind too much. We had only been in the hotel for a year when things started to get bad. We started getting aggro from Julie's dad and two brothers. They kept coming around demanding that I pay for things like the water bills and BT bills for the old house because Julie couldn't afford to pay them.

When I refused to comply with their demands, I was threatened with violence every time.

After six months or so of this, Sue and I decided to move up to Sue's hometown of Rugby in Warwickshire. Sue got in touch with her mum and dad to see if we could stay with them. They said it was OK, so we moved up there in March 1982. We told the hotel that we had to go up there in an emergency.

Chapter 16
Moving on with Friend's

I packed a few things and left, not knowing where I was going to stay that night, and I didn't care either. I went up to the High Street for a coffee, and there I bumped into Dave and Les. I told them what had happened, and they told me to come home with them and that I could stay as long as I needed to. So, I stayed at their house for about 11 months.

During that time, I was not in the right frame of mind. I just couldn't get my head around what had happened in the last few months. As hard as I tried to understand the reasons why, I just couldn't. It was while I was in this unstable state of mind that one day, Dave had gone out, and Lesley and I were at home alone. Les made me a coffee in the kitchen and then came over to give me a hug. She was big on making people feel loved, and I was no exception, but this time was different from any other time. Les told me that she fancied me something rotten.

I said that I felt much the same way, but I hadn't done anything about it because of Dave being a mate. I was still very much confused about how I felt, but I went with my gut feeling. Les and I kissed for the first time in the kitchen, and it quickly turned into a bit of a grope. Just then, Dave came back through the back gate and saw us in the kitchen. He came through the back door and said to Lesley, "If you don't want me and you want Brian instead, I'll leave," and then he left, leaving us alone.

At that time, Lesley had one child, Gavin, who was seven months old. I decided to start a new relationship with Les; it seemed like the right thing to do at the time, although I was still grieving for the loss of Gemma and my dad.

We went into the front room, sat down, and talked for a long time. We spent the afternoon watching a video on the sofa. Once Gavin had been fed and gone to bed for the night, Les put clean sheets on the bed and told me to relax, assuring me that we'd be fine. Then we went to bed, but this time, to sleep. We were both well and truly knocked out.

About eight months later, Les kicked me out onto the street. Nothing new there, then. I'd been there so many times before, but this time, I had lost so much of my own personal things that I could never replace. Nothing of great value, but of great sentimental value to me.

I went back to Eastbourne to look up some good friends of mine, Rick and Audrey. I told them what had happened, but they couldn't help me at the time. I told them not to worry; I'd find a place at a friend's house. But I didn't have anywhere else to try. I was running out of options. It was now looking more likely that I was going to become homeless for the first time in my life.

Chapter 17
Experiencing Homelessness

I went to a café for a coffee and a bite to eat, and had a long, hard think about the predicament I was in. After an hour in the café, I went down to the seafront to find somewhere to sleep for the night.

I ended up at the other end of the seafront, at Hollywell, where there was a large shelter in a half-moon shape. At both ends of the shelter, there were large glass panels, which I thought would offer some shelter from the wind and rain.

It was getting dark, and there was no one about. That day, I had been given a blanket by the Salvation Army, but I hadn't let on that I had once been in the Army myself when I was a child.

It was an eerie place to be at night, but I had no option but to stick it out for the time being until I could sort myself out. Overnight, I heard all the sounds of the animals that lived in the surrounding woodland. It got a bit chilly, but I curled up on the bench in the corner by the glass; it wasn't as draughty there. Eventually, I drifted off to sleep.

The next day, I woke to the sound of birds in the trees, as you do first thing in the morning. I needed a wee, and since there was still no one around, I went to the back of the shelter. There was a bank at the back, with trees growing there, so I knew that if anyone was walking their dog, they wouldn't see me.

After feeling better for that, I was thirsty and hungry. I'd kept a bottle of Coke from the day before, so that was the start of my breakfast, along with a couple of roll-ups. I'd switched to roll-ups as they were cheaper than tailor-made cigarettes.

I then gathered all my things and started the long walk back down the seafront to where all the cafés were. On the way, I saw some more homeless people still asleep. I just walked on by and thought to myself that I wasn't as alone as I had first thought last night in the shelter. On the way to the café, I did a lot of thinking about what I was going to do next, but first, the only thing on my mind was having a cooked breakfast.

I arrived at the café and sat down with a large coffee while I waited for my breakfast. As I did, a woman came in who I had seen on the beach down by the pier for years, sleeping rough. She was known as Staler, the bag lady. No one seemed to know much about her, just that she had been living on the beach for about 30 years.

Just then, my breakfast arrived, and I tucked in, enjoying every mouthful. After a second cup of coffee, I went on my way, looking for a place to stay for the second night of homelessness. I had decided that it was safer to sleep in different places each night.

That night, I slept in the back of the Co-Op in town, and so it went on for the next seven months. One day, I went to sit under the pier for a while, which was close to where Staler was. By this time, I had long hair, a beard, and was looking very scruffy and dirty. I didn't have any hope for a better life. I felt doomed to a life of homelessness, and it was getting late to find a new place to sleep for the night.

Just then, Staler came back to her home-made place on the beach, under a wooden marquee, where she had slept for years. Staler had seen me around for some time, up and down the seafront. She got up and came over to me and said, "Would you like a cup of tea?"

I looked at her and said, "Are you sure you can spare it?" thinking that she was as skint as I was. She replied, "Come on then, don't be silly. I wouldn't offer if I couldn't afford it."

So I went over to what was better known as Staler's place. When I got there, I was very surprised to see how well-organised she was. She had a cooker, kettle, saucepans, and everything she needed to survive.

Staler asked me why I was homeless, so I told her all about it—about Gemma and my dad dying on the same day. Staler listened to my story and didn't interrupt once. When I finished, I asked her why she had been on the beach for all these years.

Staler replied, "You look like an honest person who has just fallen on hard times. I'll tell you my reasons if you promise not to repeat it to anyone."

I promised I wouldn't say a word to anyone, and so Staler began to tell me that she couldn't stand living in houses or enclosed spaces. That's why she had been on the beach all these years. She then told me that she wasn't short of a bob or two. In fact, she was a millionaire, with properties all over Sussex. I was astounded at what she had just told me.

I stayed on the beach that night with Staler—not sleeping together, just on the same beach. The next day, at 4 a.m., just as every day of her life, Staler had a bath in the sea. She thought I was still asleep, but I saw her on the shoreline, taking all her clothes off and getting into the sea. She washed her hair in the sea as well. When she had finished and got dressed again, I waited until she was back up the top of the beach, then pretended that I had just woken up.

Staler asked me if I had seen anything. I said, "No, seen what?" She replied, "Never mind, it doesn't matter. Do you want to go for some breakfast?"

I said, "I don't have much money."

"That's OK," she said. "I'll buy your breakfast."

At breakfast, we had a full English with all the trimmings. After we had eaten, Staler told me that the reason she lived on the beach was because, during the war, her husband had been in the Navy, and one day his ship was torpedoed and he never came back. But apart from that, as she had told me on the beach, she couldn't stand being indoors—she preferred the open doors.

There was one other thing she was going to tell me, but I wasn't to say anything to a living soul. That was that she was, in fact, a landlord and owned a number of properties all over Sussex. Since I seemed to be a nice person, she wanted to help me out with a room that she would rent to me on the cheap, to get me started. I was gobsmacked by what she had just told me, and said, "Thank you very much."

The next day, we went to a house and Staler showed me a bedsit with a bed, kitchen, and en-suite bathroom—all for just £5.7/- a week. I, of course, accepted and moved in the next day.

After a couple of months, I started to sort myself out and got a job on the bins. It was a dirty job, but the money was good, and I felt a lot better for it. Things were coming together after all this time, thanks to Staler's kindness.

One day, Staler sent me a letter asking me to meet her in a café. The letter was pushed under my door. I wasn't sure what to think, but I went off to the café to meet her. When I got there, Staler was sitting with a man. For a moment, I thought her husband had come back. I didn't ask; I thought better of it.

Staler told me to get a coffee, so I did, then went over to the table and sat down. Staler introduced me to the man as her agent, and from now on, he would be collecting the rent on a weekly basis. She said

I shouldn't look so worried; he didn't bite. I just said, "Thank goodness for that," shook his hand, and told Staler that I was now working. I asked if it meant the rent would go up.

Staler said, "Oh no, nothing like that. It just means my agent will pick up the rent instead of the way we had arranged before."

I told Staler all about how I had been getting on with the other tenants and my new job. Staler said I was looking a lot better than I was three months ago—smarter, and that it was nice to see I had done something with my beard.

The next year was to be the turning point in my life. I had made my mind up to stay on my own, work hard, and get some money behind me for a rainy day.

I stayed in the bedsit for the next four years, and during that time, my brother Kevin didn't know that I had been homeless, or that a stranger—Staler—had helped me out when my own brother wouldn't put me up when I needed it most.

So, I made my mind up then. If I was ever in a position to be much better off and Kevin was in financial trouble, I wouldn't help him.

I knew this was wrong to feel, but I couldn't help it. If that was to be the way of things, then so be it. But at the same time, I would never fall out with Kevin over it—that wasn't the way I was with others. And that included Kevin, or Mr Goody Two-Shoes, as I called him.

Chapter 18
My 2nd Marriage

It was now 1984, time for the next stage of my life to begin. I went to the cinema one night. I had gone quite often in 1983 and 1984, just for something to do, and one of the ushers had caught my eye. She had been giving me the look for a while, so I asked her out for a drink. By this time, I had my own flat in Willingdon, near Polegate. We went out for a drink, and I dropped Julie off just around the corner from her home. We met a few days later in town for coffee and went for a walk in the park.

Julie told me that her dad was an evil, vindictive man, and she could not have a boyfriend. If he knew, he would beat her up.

Some weeks later, I was invited to meet Julie's parents and was invited to tea. The day came, and we arrived. Julie's dad was sitting in his armchair, watching TV. The cricket was on, and all he could say was, "Hello, have a seat. Do you like cricket?" I said no—that was the wrong answer, but I didn't know it at the time.

Months later, Julie and I were back at the flat talking about moving in together. We knew it wasn't going to be easy. We went back to Julie's mum and dad's, and Julie told them. Julie's dad went ballistic, threw me out, and told me not to call again. I sat in the car for a few minutes, and it was then that I heard the screams coming from the house.

I decided to call the police. The phone box was just down the road and around the corner from the house. The police told me to go back to the house and wait outside for them to arrive. When I got back to the house, I saw Julie's dad looking out of the window. He then came out of the front door and shouted at me to go.

I got out of the car, stood by the front of the car, leaned against it, folded my arms, and stared at him. Just then, the police arrived. I told them what had been going on, and they went inside to give Julie the chance to do what she wanted—to go with me or stay at home. About half an hour went by, and the front door opened. Julie and one of the policewomen came out. The police came over to the car and said that they would give us a one-hour start to get well away, and off we went. We took a drive to Hastings for coffee and to take time to calm down.

When we arrived in Hastings, we went to the café at the other end of the seafront. I got two takeaway coffees, and we sat on the beach and talked for a long time. Then we went back to the flat, where we had dinner. Julie settled in that night, and we just went to bed and fell asleep. In the morning, Julie told me how evil her dad was to her all the time. I told her not to worry—things would calm down, and we should get on with our lives now. She agreed, so we started to sort things out for ourselves.

We stayed in that flat for another eight months, then moved into town. There, we had a big room with a coal fire. We would go over to the park at night and get old tree branches for the fire. We had to share the kitchen with the other tenants, but the kitchen was next to our room, which was handy for us.

A few months later, Julie found out she was expecting a baby. We thought long and hard about how we were going to tell her parents. We rang her mum and told her over the phone. At this point, they had no idea where we had been living.

She said that we could come around for tea one day, and she would tell Julie's dad and tell him to stay calm. We went to see them on the day. You could cut the atmosphere with a knife. We stayed for as long as we could, but we didn't tell them that we were just about to be evicted, along with all the other tenants, as the landlord was planning to immigrate to Canada in the new year of 1982.

The council re-housed us in a one-bedroom flat in Hampden Park. The flat was an upstairs maisonette. We had almost managed to get it redecorated in time for the wedding. We got married three months before Terry was born. The wedding went surprisingly smoothly, and I was very pleased that my mum could come all the way from Darlington. The reception was held in a marquee in Julie's back garden.

After the reception, we went back to the flat, where Julie had something planned for me. I couldn't think what it could be. The only thing I could think of was the one room we hadn't decorated yet!

We got back to the flat on our own. It was a very hot summer that year, and my thoughts were right. Julie asked me if I wanted to finish the decorating in the front room. "Yes," I said, "if you're up to it." Julie said, "Only with no clothes on." "Yes," I said. We moved all the furniture into the middle of the room, laid down the dust sheets, and then Julie said, "I think we'd better put down some plastic sheets as well."

We got all the paint out, and the rollers and brushes. Julie said she would put the paint on the roller while I painted the ceiling. I got up the ladder, and we started. We had got about halfway across the ceiling when I turned around on the ladder, and Julie, on purpose, painted me with the roller.

I said, "I'll get you back for that." So, when we were doing the walls, I got paint all down her front. We carried on until we had finished it all. We went into the bathroom first to clean the brushes, and then to clean ourselves. By the time we had cleaned up, it was nearly 3 a.m., and we just flopped into bed.

Three months later, Julie went into labour, and I took her to the DGH in Eastbourne. Julie was in labour for three days and nights before Terry was born. I stayed with her the whole time. I was as knackered as Julie, with just coffee to drink and nothing to eat.

But it was well worth it. I wouldn't have missed it for the world. It was truly amazing to see it all.

I went back home that night, totally knackered. I got a takeaway on the way back home and had it delivered. Then I went to bed. The next morning, I had a long bath and went back to the DGH in the afternoon.

When I got to the hospital and onto the ward, the nurse told me that the doctor wanted to see Julie and me for a chat. We waited until the doctor came on his rounds. When he came to us, he told us that Terry had a mild form of Terry's Syndrome but that there was nothing to worry about—it would be hardly noticeable later in his life.

Two weeks later, I took Julie and Terry home. We were still living in the one-bedroom flat, and by this time, Julie's mum and dad had found out where we were living. Things weren't too bad, but I still didn't trust him as far as I could spit. He was still as evil as he always was, and his wife couldn't do anything to stop him.

Julie and I got on with our lives the best we could for the next two years. In that time, we moved into a three-bedroom house in what was the village of Langney, which was now part of Eastbourne. The house had a porch at the front door, a front room, kitchen/dining room, downstairs toilet, three bedrooms upstairs, a bathroom, and small front and back gardens. The back of the house faced onto the crematorium, but we could only see it from the back bedroom windows through the tall trees.

Shortly after that, I went self-employed as a painter and decorator, building maintenance, and roofing contractor. I enjoyed my work until my partner took on a £15,000 contract that he couldn't complete on time. So, we went bankrupt, and that was that.

Then, I got Julie pregnant again, but this time, things went well with the pregnancy, and Kimberley was born. By the time Kimberley was six months old, things were getting very bad with all the aggravation Julie and I were having to put up with from Julie's dad. He just wouldn't let up until we split up. Julie and I loved each other very deeply, and the only thing that was driving a wedge between us was Julie's dad and her three older brothers—all as bad as her dad.

I didn't stand a chance of keeping Julie safe and away from her dreaded father and all the evil things he did to split us up. Well, it wasn't much longer before his wishes came true. A few months later, Julie and I unfortunately split up, all because Julie's dad wouldn't leave things alone. But that's all he ever did, all the time.

Julie and I decided that we would always remain good friends, just for the kids at the very least.

I was devastated and found it very hard to come to terms with—losing Gemma from my first marriage, and now Terry and Kimberley from my second marriage. I moved out and went back into a B&B just down the road from Eastbourne Pier, where I lived for a while.

I had been staying at the hotel for about five months when I was offered a small gardening job. The only catch was that I had to bring my own tools. My tools were at Julie's house, so I rang her to ask if I could get them back. Julie said it was fine, and the next day, I was having coffee in my room with a friend when there was a knock at the door.

I opened the door, and to my horror, Julie's dad and three of her brothers were standing there. Julie's dad was holding my garden fork and said, "You want your tools? Well, here they are." Without another word, he stabbed me in the foot with the fork. He then told me to stay away from his daughter and never see his children again.

I didn't see my children for a long time after that. But twelve months later, I got in touch with Julie to tell her that I had found someone new and was planning to move away. I didn't want Julie's dad to know where I was going before I left, so I kept the location to myself.

Julie and I met on the beach, and she had the children with her. We spent the day together, and that was the last time I saw my children. I was devastated. But my new partner, Sue, reassured me that she would never do something like that to me. Her words made me feel a lot better. Sue was four months pregnant.

Sue told me that she had called her parents, and they had offered for us to stay with them until I found a new job in Rugby, where there were plenty of opportunities. Sue's parents didn't think it would take me long to get one.

Chapter 19
Moving to Rugby

When we arrived at the train station in Rugby, we were met by Bob, Sue's dad. He was a ginger-haired man with a walking stick. Bob took us to the house, which was on an estate called Tin Town. It was called that because the top half of the houses were covered in tin. When we arrived, I could see what Bob meant. Still, we went in, and I met Sue's mum, Margaret. She was disabled, as Bob was, but they were both Christians and went to church on Sundays. We all sat down, had a cup of tea, and chatted about what had happened in Eastbourne before we left. Bob and Margaret were amazed at how I had managed to keep my temper and stay so cool, calm, and collected for so long.

Two weeks later, Bob said that if we were going to be staying for good, it was time we got the rest of our things from the Eastbourne hotel. He arranged for a friend of his to take me back to Eastbourne to do the pick-up. When we got back to the hotel and went through reception, we were stopped by the receptionist, who asked for the rent. I told her I would go to the bank first thing in the morning and get the money.

The next day came, and at about 6am, we loaded up the van and went back to the room for a coffee. After that, we went back downstairs, and by that time, the receptionist was back on duty. I told her I was just going to the bank to get the money and that I would be back soon.

We got back in the van and drove back to Rugby. I had no intention of paying the hotel.

When we arrived back in Rugby and unloaded all our belongings into the outhouse, they were stored there for the next two months. After that, Bob said that if we were going to settle in Rugby for good, it was time I got a job. So, I did just that. I went up to the town to the job centre and found a job working as a cleaner in a big factory, ready to start the following Monday morning.

I went back to Bob and Margaret and told them about the job. I also mentioned that it was paid monthly. They said that was fine, and when I got my first wages, we could start paying a bit of housekeeping money. We went to put our names on the housing list, but there was an eight-year waiting list.

Every day, I went up to the job centre to look for work. This went on for several weeks until one day, I went up to the job centre and came back with a job. I went for the interview and was told I could start the following Monday. I went back home and told Bob and Margaret. They were pleased for me but said they were beginning to think I was lazy and didn't want to work.

Chapter 20
The Foundry & Accident

I started work and was shown around the factory. There were lots of places to clean all over the site. I was also told that when I was in the foundry and a slinger told me to stand still, I had to do just that. We gradually worked our way through the foundry, cleaning as we went. We went through the foundry and on to the moulding shop. When we got back into the foundry, we were told to stop where we were, as they were about to pour 120 tons of molten metal into two huge runners. The molten metal would run down two long runners and into the mould, which was in a big pit.

I asked what was being made in the mould. "It's part of a coal crusher used in the coal industry," I was told. "Oh," I replied.

After the job was poured and the giant ladles had been taken back to the scrap metal end of the foundry, we all went back to work.

Quite some weeks later, when I had been working as a cleaner in the foundry, I spotted a job that was advertised on the internal notice board for a serviceman. I filled in an application form and got the job. It paid a lot more than I was getting at the time—over £125 a week more. In my new job, I had to clean up after the moulders and do all the bolting up of the jobs, getting them ready for casting. The slingers would then get the crane to pick the whole job up and place it in the spot where it was going to be cast.

The foundry was split into different bays, and while I was working in these different bays, I kept a very close eye on how the slingers did their job, as that was what I really wanted to do. In the meantime, I had to get on with all the duties in the foundry. For example, when a job had cooled down enough, we had to take out all the metal rods, which were still black hot, and we had to wear special safety gloves that were heat resistant. The heat and dust were horrendous.

After we had taken all the rods out, the slinger had to pull the job out using the crane. The job was then left for the next two or three days to cool completely before it was sent to the fettling shop to be cleaned up before the ship's sump went off to its destination. The old sand left in the moulding boxes went off to the shocker, where the burnt sand was shaken out and re-used.

A few months later, I went in for my slinger's training and passed the test with a high safety score. I was then able to work as a slinger, on my own, with my own crane driver.

Sometime later, for the first time, I had to pick up and turn over five LR18s, which were 12ft by 12ft boxes bolted together, full of hard sand and half of a mould. The other half was on the moulding bed. First, I had to pick it up and take it to the gangway, resting it down on large wooden blocks on one end. I then had to take the hooks off and put them on one end of the job. When the gangway was clear of people walking through, I told the crane driver to hoist the job up slowly, and then stand the job up on one end.

I then had to climb up on top of the job and move the hooks to the other side of what was now the top of the job. After that, I climbed back down and told the crane driver to lift the job up very slowly so it didn't start to swing. I then moved the job over to the other side of the gangway and turned it over, so the job was now upside down. I unhooked the job, re-hooked it, and held it over the other half of the job while the moulder put the sealing clay on the join. Once this was done, I placed the job on the casting bed.

About 18 months later, money was getting a bit tight at home. By this time, I had two more kids: Christian, who was 4 years old, and Zara, who was 2 and a half. Sue, who was never satisfied with the wages I was bringing home, even though I was bringing home £285 a week, was still not happy.

I saw the chance to go on nights at work. The money was considerably higher than the day shift, so I started doing nights at a wage of £350 a week, plus danger money of £150 a week, bringing my total to £500 a week take-home pay. And still, she wasn't satisfied. This made me very angry to the point where I was finding it hard to concentrate on my job as well as I should have.

As a slinger, if I had something like a bad cold or the flu, I could take time off with full pay for one week to get over it, so I used that excuse to take time out and get my head back together.

When I went back to work, I was cleared by the foundry's medical staff to continue working. I went back on nights. I had new gloves, but they were too big. I complained about it, but I was told to make do or not use them, so I just made do. I kept working hard, as I always did.

Several months later, we had been very busy for the last three weeks, working every night. One night, my regular crane driver was off sick, and the crane driver I was given had only just passed his test. He was a bit green, to say the least. He had been working hard all night, but wasn't concentrating on the signals I had been giving him.

In the early hours of the morning, just after 4:15 a.m., I had to lift off the bogey a stack of LR5s. Because the stack of boxes was so high, I needed someone on the other side to hook up while I controlled the chains. I signalled to the crane driver to raise the hoist a touch. This meant the chains would go up slowly, so at a specific point, I could do it safely, as I had done hundreds of times before with my own crane driver.

But this time, with my regular crane driver off on holiday for two weeks, the new crane driver made a mistake. Instead of lifting the job slowly as I had instructed, he hoisted it up very fast. This meant I didn't have time to take my hands out from between the chains. My left hand became trapped between the chains and the boxes, lifting me off the floor. My left boot got caught in the metalwork of the bogey.

Despite the pain, I managed to give the signal to drop the job, and for once, the crane driver did exactly as he was told. I fell to the floor, holding my left hand to my chest and my right hand holding my left leg.

I was in excruciating pain and was taken to the hospital in an ambulance. At the hospital, I was checked over and told I had a split muscle in my right leg and would need a walking stick for the next 12 months. My left arm would be weaker than it was before.

I left the hospital and took a long, slow walk back home, thinking that my working life was over. It took me nearly two hours to get home. When I arrived at the gate of our house, Sue was looking out of the window, wondering where I had got to so late after my shift.

When Sue saw me with a walking stick, she rushed to the front door and asked what on earth had happened on my night shift. I told her all about it over a coffee. At first, Sue did everything she could to make me comfortable, but this wasn't to last long. Nine weeks later, things started to change.

By this time, I had been through two courses of physiotherapy treatment, but there was no improvement in my arm. It was still as bad as before, and I was still unable to use it much. As a last resort, the hospital decided to try a different type of physiotherapy: electronic pulse treatment.

I went for the treatment, which meant that electronic pulses were sent through my arm for up to an hour at a time. However, this didn't help either. In fact, it made things worse. After 18 months of trying physiotherapy, I was left with a walking stick and an arm/hand that still didn't function properly. I thought that this could be my life from now on.

Sue and I went to church every Sunday with her mum and dad. Three or four weeks after my physiotherapy treatment ended, I began to notice that Sue was changing towards me. She was spending more time at church functions. At first, I didn't think much of it, but it soon became clear that there was something going on between Sue and a male Sunday school teacher.

Sue went bright red when she realised she'd been found out. She tried to apologise, but I told her the damage had already been done and we could never go back to the way things were. I became very depressed because I hadn't worked for so long.

One day, Sue came back home with the Sunday school teacher for a coffee. While they were having coffee, Dave, the teacher, suggested I go back to Eastbourne for a two-week holiday to catch up with old friends and take a break from the situation. He thought it would help me feel better. After a day or two, I agreed that it was a good idea, and two weeks later, I went back to Eastbourne, or so I thought, for a break.

I took the train and called my brother, Kevin, to see if I could stay with him for a few days. Kevin told me he'd meet me at Eastbourne station. When I arrived, he told me he couldn't put me up and that I would have to find somewhere else to stay. Kevin and I went for a coffee at the station while I thought about where I could stay. After a while, I decided to call Dave and Kim, and they said I could stay with them.

When I arrived at Dave and Kim's, they told me I could stay as long as I wanted, but I'd have to sleep on the sofa. I agreed and told them everything that had been going on in my life over the last five years since I left Rugby.

But just five days later, I received a letter from Sue, dated the day after I arrived in Eastbourne. It said: "Do not bother coming back to Rugby. My new boyfriend has moved in, and I am not to be contacted again. You are not to get in touch with Christian or Zara." I was devastated by the letter, and so were Kim and Dave.

I stayed at Kim and Dave's for nearly six months before moving out to a flat in the centre of Eastbourne. During that time, I had to go to Nottingham for a medical, and on the way back, Kevin and I stopped by my old house to collect as many of my personal belongings as we could fit into Kevin's car. We then returned to Eastbourne.

My relationship with Sue ended, and I was heartbroken. I had already lost two children when I moved to Rugby, and now I had lost two more, including Christian and Zara. In total, that made five children. I couldn't stand it any longer. That's when I decided enough was enough. I was going to live on my own from now on.

Kim and Dave were incredibly supportive over the next six months. If it hadn't been for them, I would have cracked up for good. Once I came to terms with everything, I moved into a place of my own.

Chapter 21
Staying on My Own

A few weeks later, I received my compensation from the accident: £4,574.03. This paid off all the debts that my ex had put me in, as well as the ones I had, and allowed me to get a flat of my own. So, I was on my own again – so what's new?

I thought long and hard about what I was going to do with my life. After a day or two, I decided to live my life on my own and never trust a woman again. I was feeling very lonely and distressed, but things were going to change for the better in the not-too-distant future, though I didn't know that at the time.

As the weeks went on, I got my life back on track. I started to get myself organised to live on my own. My money was very short, and I was finding it hard to make ends meet, but I was managing to eat, though not very well. I wasn't too bothered, because the way I looked at it, there were a lot more people in the world who were a lot worse off than me.

I had now settled into my new studio flat for the last two months and had just gotten used to my new way of life when I went to see

Babs, my adopted niece. She invited me to stay for dinner, and I knew it would be huge, as Babs didn't do small meals. In her mind, there was no such thing.

I sat down for a coffee and watched a film with Babs's partner, Tom. I didn't like Tom that much, but I just tolerated him, as he was on drugs, and that wasn't my thing at all.

I went to Babs's flat for dinner, and she had a friend of a friend there called Nikki. She made me a coffee and handed it to me. All I said was "Cheers," not even looking at her. Nikki said to Babs that she thought I was an arrogant pig. Babs explained just what had happened to me in the not-too-distant past.

While I was waiting for my coffee, there was a young woman there – Nikki. She brought my coffee in, and all I could say was "Cheers" as Nikki handed me the cup.

Nikki went back into the kitchen where she was helping Babs with dinner, and asked Babs who the man was sitting in the corner of the front room. Babs told Nikki all about me and what I had been through in my life.

Chapter 22
Starting a New Life Together

After dinner, I went back home and walked Nikki to the bus stop. We got talking on the way, and Nikki and I arranged to see each other the following weekend. A couple of days later, Nikki and I went for a long walk along the seafront. By the time we had walked to Hollowell and back, we knew just about everything there was to know about each other. We decided to think about moving in together.

A couple of weeks later, I went to help Nikki move out of her home. Her mother was supposed to be ill in bed!

When we arrived, Nikki showed me to the front room and made me a coffee while she packed. I played with the dog – they had a Yorkshire Terrier. We had decided to tell Nikki's mum that Nikki was starting a new job as a nanny the next day, but she was moving in with me. Anyway, I could hear Nikki's mum upstairs moaning about how ill she was. When Nikki told her that I was downstairs, her mum shot out of bed and came rushing down the stairs to see me. She said that if the job didn't work out, Nikki wasn't moving in with me. I told her I was just helping Nikki take her stuff to where she was going to be working. Nikki's mum said, "That's all right then." I cracked a joke with her, and she was in stitches.

We walked up to the shopping centre, got the bus back into town, and then back to the flat.

I made dinner that night, and we had a good laugh over it all. Nikki told me how her mum always played on being ill all the time, but all she had was tinnitus, which is to do with the ears, and a simple operation would sort it out.

Later that night, Nikki thought that at 10 pm, it was bedtime, but I told her we could go to bed whenever we wanted. There was a film on TV that I wanted to watch, and it didn't finish until 1 am, so we stayed up to watch it together.

In the next few months, Nikki and I settled in together very well. We got ourselves into a good routine with the shopping and the money side of things.

Eighteen months later, we got our first council flat in Langney. It was an upstairs flat with its own garden at the back, complete with our own washing line that we didn't have to share with anyone else. It was great to have a place of our own with no noisy neighbours. We settled into our new flat and were very happy there, except for the constant interference from Sandy, Nikki's mum. I had been down that road before with my second marriage, and I wasn't going to go down that road again.

In November 1994, we found out that Nikki was pregnant. We were over the moon about it. Nikki went to the phone box and told her mum the good news. When Nikki told Sandy that she was pregnant, her mum replied, "So you've had SEX then?" When Nikki came back and told me what her mum had said, we'll never forget my reaction: "Dorr! Dip-stick! Of all the stupid things to say."

In August 1995, Nikki was diagnosed with having pre-eclampsia and was rushed to a hospital in Kent. Aaron was born by caesarean two days later. He was just 1lb 9oz.

I rang Sandy in Eastbourne and told her. She came up to Kent to see him. By this time, Aaron was in intensive care. When Sandy arrived, I took her to the intensive care unit and to the washroom. While we were in the washroom, I said to Sandy, "It's only fair to warn you, Aaron is very small, and his head is only the size of the top of a coffee cup."

As usual, Sandy knew better than I did – or so she thought. I answered with, "Well, don't say that I didn't warn you." When we got to Aaron's incubator, I looked at Sandy's face, and the look of sheer shock and horror was unmistakable. I then said, "I told you so."

A week after Aaron had died, Sandy came to see us, and Nikki was still lying on the sofa. Sandy reckoned Nikki should have been up and about by now and not lounging around on the sofa. I told Sandy to back off. She took offence because she couldn't get her way, as usual, so I chose to ignore her. She went off in a huff, huffing and puffing as she went.

At Aaron's funeral, Sandy didn't offer Nikki any comfort. During the funeral, as we walked down into the cemetery, Sandy just kept looking at all the other graves and paid no attention to what was going on. All I could think of was that Sandy was self-centred and only cared about number one: Sandy, Sandy, Sandy, and no one else.

Just three weeks later, she came to see us and said, "You should be over him by now."

I kicked her out, and she went away crying. I said, "That's tough," as she left. "You should be more caring where your daughter is concerned," I added, slamming the door behind her.

We were still grieving for the loss of our son, and all that woman could think about was herself – Sandy, Sandy, Sandy, and no one else.

When I went back into the flat, Nikki and I had a long talk about the way Sandy treated her and how she always picked holes in everything that Nikki and I did. So, we decided to take no notice of the cow.

We went out for a slap-up meal in town just to make ourselves feel better about things. After dinner, we went for a walk along the seafront and stopped for a coffee on the way back home.

We were very happy together, and that's the way we intended it to stay, no matter what the in-laws thought of us or the way we were living our lives. We were happy, and that's all that mattered.

Chapter 23
Getting Married For The 3rd Time.

I went back up to the flat, and Nikki was crying. After some time, Nikki calmed down, and we decided to try to ignore Sandy and her stupid ways. As for the comments she came out with, saying how she thought she knew it all, we just had to brush them off.

The trauma of the last two years had been too much for both of us, so we put in for a transfer with the council to a ground-floor flat. It took just four months for the council to find us a new one. During the time we had been waiting for a move, we had seen an empty flat near Langney Shopping Centre.

Five years later, Nikki and I decided to get married. However, the aggravation with Sandy flared up again. Little did we know then, but if we had known then what we know now, we would have gotten married in private.

What you are about to read is a true account of what happened.

We went to see Sandy and Frank and told them that we had decided to get married. Frank said that it didn't matter what the cost was; he would pay for it. Sandy said that she would chip in and give us all the help we needed. We just sat there gobsmacked, all we could say was, "Thank you very much."

We found a second-hand wedding dress for £50.00. We told Sandy and Frank about it, but two weeks later, Frank said that was too expensive, and they would find a cheaper one. Nikki and I went away that day, both of us thinking, "What a skinflint."

It was then that we decided to do as much as we could for ourselves. An old friend of Nikki's did flower arranging, so we rang her up. She remembered what Sandy was like from when she and Nikki were little girls. She told me all about it, and it made perfect sense. But as time went on, I was soon to find out for myself.

Nikki wanted red roses in the bouquet with white carnations, but when we showed Sandy, she said she didn't like the red roses and that we would have to cut them out. We were most put out by the way Sandy reacted to everything we came up with. Frank had found a dressmaker, so Sandy arranged the first fitting. I took Nikki to the house where the dressmaker lived and waited outside in the car. When Nikki and Sandy came out, I could see by the look on Nikki's face that Sandy had been a pain in the ass. Sandy was full of herself, saying, "I want this and I want that." I thought, "Oh, here we go again." By the way, the price of the wedding dress was to be only £350.00. Yes, that's really cheaper than the £50.00 for the second-hand dress—hardly.

Sandy insisted on how the dress was going to look, and Nikki wasn't going to have a say in it. For the second fitting, we told Sandy the wrong day on purpose, so she wouldn't be there when Nikki went for the fitting. The dressmaker said, "Now, how do you want the dress to look? It's your day, not your mother's day. I will not listen to mothers. It's up to you only."

The dress was changed beyond recognition. Nikki had the neckline made lower, added pearls, lace sleeves, and a shawl—it was just the way Nikki wanted it to be.

We left the wedding rings down to Sandy to get, as that was something she wanted to do, so we gave in on that one just to keep the peace. Margery, my sister-in-law who runs the café at the charity shop, offered to do the catering for the wedding. But even that was considered too expensive and not the right type of food to eat. There were no gateaux, and we just had to have them, even though I don't eat them because of the migraines I suffer from. So, as with everything else, Sandy and Frank went elsewhere.

A very good friend of ours said that she was willing to do the cars with ribbons for us as one of our wedding presents. Carol told Sandy and Frank that on the day, she would come up to their flat at 10am to decorate their car. But when Carol got there, Frank was out with the car. Carol was fuming. Frank came back home at 10:45am—just one hour and fifteen minutes before the wedding—and I had to get changed. Sandy and Frank, to make matters worse, lived at the other side of town. I rushed back home, got changed, and then went off to the town hall. Just before Nikki left Sandy and

Frank's, Carol wanted to take some photos of the bride and Frank, but it took three attempts to get him to pose for a photo.

On the day of the wedding at the Town Hall, all the guests had arrived. We had invited over 90 guests, and 62 of them had come to the Town Hall. Nikki arrived looking radiant but anxious. Nikki and I went into the registrar's office for a final chat before we went up for the ceremony. We needed the extra calm time to settle down. It was a very hot day, and I was sweating already—I wasn't used to a shirt and tie.

When we were ready, we went up the stairs to the room where we were to be married. When we got to the door, the first person we saw was Sandy, making a big deal out of fanning herself with the program, while everyone else was just standing around in the heat, waiting for us to enter the room. We took our places in front of the registrar and began to say our wedding vows. As I was saying mine, I could just hear Sandy in the background moaning about the heat. For once, I was thinking the same thing. By this time, the sweat was pouring off me, and I was beginning to feel a bit dizzy, but I thought, "If I can just hang on a bit longer, the wedding part is nearly over, and soon we'll be outside in the shade on the Town Hall steps." We went for a long kiss when the registrar said, "You may kiss the bride," and then we made our way back down the stairs, having our photos taken on the way down. When we got down to the Town Hall steps, the cool breeze was refreshing.

After that, Carol took us to the pub gardens at the Lamb Inn in Old Town for a drink and some private photos, while the rest of the guests went back to Sandy and Frank's for a cold buffet. I didn't know then, but my side of the family hadn't been invited. We stayed for over 60 minutes at the Lamb Inn. Carol had gotten us a bottle of real champagne and two champagne flutes to keep after.

When we went back to Sandy and Frank's, it was then that we found out my family hadn't been invited, so we were not very happy about that. All Sandy was interested in was her side of the family and herself. She had invited all the residents in the flats in the block.

The chicken drumsticks were pink instead of being white, and most of the buffet had gone by the time we arrived. After the cold buffet, Nikki and I went back home and had something else to eat. We then went out to see my family for two hours before the evening disco and dance, and there was another disaster waiting to unfold.

Nikki was made very welcome in my family. The difference between the two families could not have been more stark—one side was selfish, and the other side was kind, helpful, and supportive at all times.

The Evening: Disco and Dance.

In the late afternoon, Sandy rang us to come and give a hand at the Langney Sports Club, where the evening disco was to be held. We picked up a good friend of ours, Vanessa, and her daughter, Vicki, who was helping us to get the hall ready. We all worked hard to get it set up while Sandy gave the orders. At about 4 p.m., the food arrived: meat, sausage rolls, spicy items, and the famous Gâteaux – all six of them. It was in the 90s, but Sandy insisted that the Gâteaux would be fine for the evening.

As the evening came, we entered the hall, and there was a table just inside the door with drinks for the guests to start with, before they moved on to the bar. None of my family drank alcohol. There was a main table in the middle of the floor, with tables all around the room. There was a stage with more tables, where my family sat, though we were well apart from each other. The atmosphere was so tense you could cut it with a knife on Sandy's side of the family.

As the disco went on, most of the time Sandy and her family stayed outside, talking to each other and paying no attention to my side of the family. We found out that Sandy had been in touch with most of the guests, which is why most of them didn't come for the disco. As a result, we missed out on a lot of presents that night, all because of Sandy's mouth. The food had been left in the heat for too long and was starting to spoil by the time the evening arrived. The Gâteaux were the best thing – just because Sandy insisted on six of them. It was funny; they looked just like five cow pats where the chocolate had melted. Gross!

At the end of the night, we cleaned up so Sandy wouldn't lose her precious deposit. We were just glad it was all over and we could finally go home. Thank goodness for that.

Chapter 24
Mum's 90th Surprise Birthday 2003

Two years after we got married, just after the New Year in 2003, we had a phone call from Kevin, my brother, to say that he had just received a call from Hazel, my sister in Darlington. She lives with my mum, and mum was coming up for her 90th birthday in a week's time. Hazel was planning a surprise dinner to celebrate mum's birthday in Darlington and was trying to get all the family there, if she could, as a surprise for mum. I told Kevin that I would have to look into my finances and let him know in a day or two. When I came off the phone, I told Nikki what was going on and that mum was not to know about it until the Saturday night when we would all be there at Hazel's house. I told Kevin that we would be going.

Nikki said it was up to me as I knew if we could afford to go or not. I said that the only way we could is if I could up one of my Visas by about £300. We'd see.

I thought about it long and hard for the next two days, then rang one of my Visa companies. The first one said "No," but the other one said "Yes" and said that, as I had been making regular payments for the last two years, I could have my Visa limit increased by £500 if that would help. Of course, I said yes, and the extra credit was then applied to the new limit.

I told Nikki that there was now nothing to stop us from going, except Pepe the dog.

So, we first asked Sandy and Frank, but they said "No" because of the rules where they lived. We then asked a couple of other people we knew, but they all said, for one reason or another, that they were unable to help. So, I said to Nikki, "What if we can find a hotel in Darlington that will take both us and the dog?" Nikki said that it was a long way to take the dog, as she was so young—only five months old at the time.

I did a lot of ringing around to the hotels in Darlington. I was not going to give up until I found one that would accommodate us. I eventually found one, so I sent off the deposit, and we were all set to go on the 29th of March 2003.

We had been looking forward to it for just over a month. I knew the car would be okay; we had a Motability car, and it was only two years old.

The 29th came, and we set off from Eastbourne at 9am, arriving in Darlington at about 4.30pm. When we arrived at the hotel, the room wasn't quite ready, so I took Nikki and Pepe to the South Park, where I used to play as a child. Nikki took one look at the field and said, "Look at the size of this!" I said, "This is only a quarter of the park." We stretched our legs after the long journey. I pointed out parts of the park and told Nikki all the things we used to get up to when we were kids.

We went back to the hotel, and the room was ready for us. We took our bags and Pepe's night cage up to the room. As you went through the door, the bed was on the right, just around the corner. The room was L-shaped; it had a kettle, a TV, and one single bed in the other corner of the room. We used that to put the cases on, after all, we were only there for two days, then we were going back home. The first thing we did was put the kettle on for a coffee. Pepe had a good sniff around the place. While we were having coffee, I rang Hazel to let her know that we had arrived safely. She told us to come around her house at about 7pm after we had had some dinner, as mum was going out for dinner and still had no idea what we were all up to.

We both settled in and then had a bite to eat. We had to live on takeaways while we were in Darlington, but we knew that and didn't mind for the time we were there. We went to Hazel's at 6.45pm and parked the car just up the road so mum wouldn't notice it coming back to Hazel's. We went in and sat down—Kevin and Margery, Stacy and Andrew, then Joy and Robert, our older sister, followed by Gillian and Robin, my cousin, then Nicola and her boyfriend, and last but by no means least, Rachael and her husband. The front room became full of family from all over the country. Nicola came in from the kitchen, where she had been keeping watch, and said, "Everyone quiet, they're coming." The room went deadly silent as mum and Hazel parked the car in the drive. Mum came in on her walking stick, and Hazel stood right behind her when Nicola opened the front room door. When mum saw us all sitting in Hazel's front room, she was completely gobsmacked, with the biggest smile and a tear in her eye of sheer joy, and said, "Oh my goodness, look at you all, have you come to see me?"

Looking at Nikki, me, and the rest of the family, Brian said, "And this is your new addition, what's her name?" We said, "Pepe." Mum thought we said "paper," but she soon got it right. We all had a coffee and a long chat. Mum was inundated with presents for her birthday and for Mother's Day; she was a bit overwhelmed. We made arrangements to meet the next day for the special dinner that Hazel had organised.

Hazel told us that she had arranged for a friend to look after Pepe while we went for dinner, and it was not too far from the restaurant.

We all went back to our hotels for the night. The next day, Nikki and I met at Hazel's after breakfast, so that Hazel could show us the way to the restaurant.

We followed Hazel to the restaurant, and when we arrived, we drove up the long driveway. The restaurant was set far back from the road. They had rolled out the red carpet for mum, as she is a VIP in Darlington. We walked through the marble posts and into the lounge area, then through the bar and into the restaurant. The walls were dark blue velvet, and the napkins were also velvet.

We all sat down at the long table. It was wonderful for us all to be there, after so long of living all over the country. I sat next to mum, and Nikki was next to me. Rachel sat next to mum on the other side of her. We started dinner with posh fruit in a red sauce, and for the main course, we had a choice of beef, pork, duck, venison, turkey, goose, or grouse. The meal was magnificent. The pudding was out of this world, and we had freshly ground coffee to follow.

I got a surprise when Rachel got up and asked me if I would like to go outside with her for a smoke. That made me feel so much better, as I wasn't the only one in my family who smoked after all.

After dinner, we all went off to do our own thing, and in the evening, we all met up again for mum's birthday celebrations and a buffet afterwards, to see mum cutting the cake.

The next day, we were going back home to Eastbourne via York to see Nikki's auntie. We went back to the hotel, watched a bit of TV, and then went to bed. What a great day.

The next day, we set off at 8.15am for York to see Nikki's auntie, but we missed the turning and went too far. I found a place to stop, and we rang Nikki's auntie. She said, "You've gone too far, you'd better keep going down the motorway, or you won't get back home until the early hours of the morning. Not to worry, maybe I'll see you next time."

Nikki said, "Let's go to see Leeds instead," so we did. We had a look at some of the places Nikki used to play in when she was a child, but Leeds had changed so much since Nikki was there last.

We got well and truly lost and ended up on the wrong road. But at least we were still going south.

But it was all good fun. We went to Leeds, saw Nikki's old school, and a few other places. Around lunchtime, I said to Nikki, "It's getting a bit late in the day to still be so far from home, and I'm getting a bit tired from all the driving." So, we hit the road, but again, we somehow got on the wrong motorway and ended up on the M6, still going south. So, we just kept on going. I thought that if we kept on going, we'd see a road I recognised.

As I was driving down the road, I noticed that both Nikki and the dog had fallen asleep. I took advantage of the situation, as Nikki had started to panic about the time it was taking to get back home, and the dog had been getting restless in the back of the car.

I put my foot down a bit and went 90mph to make up some time. Just over three hours later, we eventually got back home at 11.45pm, well and truly knackered.

Chapter 25
Working for the Salvation Army

In 2001, I passed my driving test even though I had a bad arm that gave me a lot of pain most of the time. But that wasn't going to stop me from doing the best I could with my life, for both myself and my wife, Nikki.

By 2006, I had been unemployed since the accident in 1990 and was feeling down in the dumps. I wasn't in control of my life, especially where money was concerned.

So, I went to the local job centre to see what opportunities were available in my area. I started looking and it wasn't long before I found six possibilities. I printed out the details for each job and arranged interviews, which kept me busy for the next week or two. Unfortunately, I had no luck with any of them. I didn't want to go back to a cleaning job because the wages were too low. I didn't think Nikki and I could survive on that kind of money, especially since we were already struggling to pay off our credit cards. The interest on them kept going up and up.

I wasn't going to be put off by all the rejection letters from potential employers. I just kept on trying, continually looking in the local papers and at the job centre. I wasn't going to give up easily. Sometimes, when I went to the job centre, there would be some scruffy young people hanging around outside with tatty jeans and messy hair. I often thought that those people didn't want to work and would never have a proper life. I thought how stupid they were being, and how much better I was than that.

Another year passed, and I was still searching hard for a job with no success. One day, I went into the job centre and saw a vacancy for a Caretaker at the Salvation Army, the same one I had attended as a child. I thought about it for a week but did nothing about it.

Two weeks later, I went back to the job centre and, to my surprise, the job was still available. I thought for a moment and realised that it was a job, and it could be a way of getting out of debt in the long term. So, I called up and arranged an interview for the next day at 10 am with Major Stuart.

The next day, I arrived at the Salvation Army at 9:45 am for the interview and met Major Stuart for the first time. During the interview, I was asked a lot of questions to see how much I knew about the job and what it entailed. Having a diploma in handling chemicals helped a lot. Part of the interview involved being shown around the premises. I told the Major that I had been brought up in the Army, so I pretty much knew my way around, but I let him show me around anyway.

After the interview, I was asked if I could start first thing in the morning at 6 am and meet the Major outside at 5:45 am. I said I could, so I arrived at 5:30 am the next day. The Major wasn't there, and didn't arrive until 5:55 am, five minutes late.

When the Major arrived, I tried to make a bit of a joke about him being late, looking at my watch and saying, "You're a bit late." The Major wasn't amused. He gave me a dirty look and said, "Don't try to be funny with me. I'm the boss." I quickly said I was only joking and didn't mean anything by it. The Major showed me where my stock was and explained how he wanted things done. I was told that I'd be working on my own from the next day onwards.

I was given a set of master keys and a swipe card for the alarm. On my first day, I was getting annoyed with the way the Major expected everything to be done immediately, as if it were all urgent.

About three weeks into the job, Maureen came in. With a surprised look on her face, she said, "I heard we had a new Hall Caretaker, but we didn't know it was you! How are you?" She also told me that the Major was leaving and moving to a new Corps (that's what the Salvation Army calls its local units). That made me feel a lot better about putting up with the current Major for the next five months. By then, I'd be well and truly settled into my role. Maureen also mentioned that not many of the people liked the current Major anyway—he was very bolshie.

I noticed that the youth hall floor wasn't as clean as it had been when I was younger, but I didn't do anything about it while the current Major was there. I figured I'd leave it for a bit, since it was the only thing the Major hadn't complained about.

The five months went by quickly, and when the new Major arrived, he was much nicer. Major David Squirrel and his wife, Major Linder, were much more understanding.

Six months after Major David had started, my brother Kevin was holding his 25th wedding anniversary at the Army Youth Hall. Nikki and I were invited, but Nikki wasn't feeling well that day, so I went on my own.

During the evening, something was spilled on the floor, and when it was cleaned up, it left a light mark. That's when I realised the floor was absolutely filthy and needed a good scrub. The next Saturday, I went into work earlier than usual, at 4 am, and managed to scrub half of the floor while also doing my other work.

On the Monday, during the parents and toddlers group, I waited for the comments. One of the women came in, saw me walking through the hall, and said, "Brian, what's happened to the floor?" I just smiled and replied, "I got down on my hands and knees and scrubbed it at 4 am this morning. I'll have to do the other half another time."

Just then, Major David came in and asked the same thing as Pat. I smiled again and said the same thing to the Major. Major David then said to me, "You're doing a wonderful job. We all say so. I've had many good comments about how clean you keep the halls. Thank you very much for all your hard work."

Hearing that made me feel so much better about the job I was doing, and it gave me the incentive to carry on. Now, people cared about the high standards of work I always strived for in all the jobs I had ever done in my life.

I loved my job because it was the same job my dad had done in the church all those years ago. And the fact that I was brought up in the Army meant so much to me.

Chapter 26
Langney Area Panel

Three years later, the Eastbourne Council sent a letter to all Eastbourne tenants, asking for people to form four panels in the town. As Nikki and I lived in the Langney part of the town, we decided to attend the meeting at the local community centre.

We went to the meeting, and there were about 20 people there. At the end of the meeting, there was a vote for the three positions to run the panels: Chairman, Secretary, and Treasurer. Both the Chairman and Secretary were voted for, but no one wanted to take on the Treasurer's job. A lot of the people there knew me, so they voted for me for the role. Nikki said she could run the office, man the phone, and co-organise things.

I had to go to a meeting with the council to be trained on the way they wanted things done. After the meeting, a bank account was opened for the Langney Area Panel, and I would oversee £23,000.00 each year to be used for all of the panel's projects throughout the year.

It was a very busy time as I had just started working for the Salvation Army two years earlier, but I knew I could give the commitment and time that was needed.

Nikki and I bent over backwards to help the public and the tenants of Eastbourne for the next 4½ years, and I thoroughly enjoyed it. Even though, at times, we went back home annoyed at the things some people expected the panel to be able to do for them. On some matters, we had our limits, although we could put pressure on the council at times—but not all the time.

We did not take petty cash for petrol or out-of-pocket expenses. At the end of each year, the books were taken for orientation, and I was always spot on with my figures.

We did all sorts of projects around our part of Eastbourne, for the common good of the community, and we took great pride in what we were doing for others.

At the end of the 4½ years on the panel, there was a new Secretary and Chairman, and things became very difficult for Nikki and me, so we both left. This was just after we had been nominated for our first Eastbourne Achiever's Award, though we didn't know it at the time, for all the hard work we had done over the past 20 years for charities.

Chapter 27
2007 Eastbourne Achievers Award

At the same time as working on the panel, we were also helping another charity, ESDA, for disabled people. We became known as the "fan-tam staffers" because of the speed at which we could stuff just over 7,500 of their magazines into envelopes for mailing. When we started doing the magazines, it took us on average 5 hours, but as time went on, we just got faster and faster. By the time we had been doing it for 3 years, we had got down to just 2½ hours. The rest of the staff at ESDA started having friendly bets on the time it would take us. Nikki and I got wind of this one day when we had finished, so the next time we went in to do the magazines, we decided to try and beat our fastest record of 2½ hours and go all out. We took in extra drinks and food so we could go as quickly as possible. While I got the magazines ready on the tables, Nikki went and made me a coffee. After that, we just drank the cold drinks we had brought in.

We did indeed beat our record that day. We finished the 7,800 magazines in just 1¼ hours, busting all of our previous records by a mile. None of the staff at ESDA could believe it. When I went out of the room and said, "We've finished," the comments from the staff were, "Good God, already?" I replied, "Yep, all done."

At that time at ESDA, two other jobs came up: one was for a gardener, and the other was for someone to check the database. With me being dyslexic, I did the gardening, and Nikki took on the database. We did that for the next 4 years, and we both thoroughly enjoyed it.

At Christmas time, ESDA had a Christmas dinner at a restaurant or hotel. It was a great time when all of the voluntary staff got to gather and let their hair down. We always made sure that those who had trouble eating received help from all of us. Some of the staff who took the phone calls in reception were either partially sighted or one of them was blind. We all did a great job for the charity.

Two more years went by when Nikki and I got a surprise. We were told that we had been nominated for an Eastbourne Achiever's Award, and the awards ceremony was going to be held at the Eastbourne Grand Hotel in two months' time. We had been invited to attend the event. I had to wear a dickie bow tie, and Nikki had to wear an evening dress.

On the evening of the awards, we got ready to go, but neither of us liked being in the limelight, let alone on a stage in front of a lot of strangers. We were both feeling pretty nervous. We drove down the Eastbourne seafront and managed to find a parking space just in front of the Grand Hotel. When we got out of the car, Nikki said,

"Off we go then," but I replied, "Not yet. I'm having a fag first." So, we stood by the car for a while as I smoked, and then we went into the hotel. We were greeted in the foyer of the Grand Hotel and shown to our seats.

There were a lot of big round tables, with 10 people on each table, and about 30 tables in total. So, there were a lot of people there, which made us even more nervous. We sat down, and at our table was a lady I had gone to school with. She had sadly lost her daughter to cancer and had started a charity in her daughter's memory.

As the evening went on and the categories were read out, it came to the category we had been nominated for, along with the other people at our table. To our surprise, we won! The panic eased a bit, and we knew we just had to face it as we went up on the stage. We shook hands, took the award, and returned to our seats with a sigh of relief. The people at our table said, "Well done."

Then we had our photos taken with the big bosses from Eastbourne Homes. It was a frantic milestone in our lives.

We had a great time that night and felt so proud of our achievement. The fact that all we had done together had not gone unnoticed is something we can't explain in words.

Just two years later, we found ourselves in the same position again, at the Grand Hotel. We had no idea it was coming, but at least this time we knew what to expect. So, now we have not one, but two awards.

Chapter 28
Not Speaking to Us

In 2009, things started to get a bit strange with Nikki's mum and dad. For years, they had been dishonest with the insurance companies they had policies with, including home insurance. One time, they asked me to drop a lighted cigarette down the side of the sofa, just because Nikki's mum didn't like the colour of it. I reminded them that all furniture was fireproof. Two weeks later, they spilled nail varnish on the arm of the sofa and got the money to buy a new one. They were always trying to get money for nothing.

Nikki's mum, like me, had been in a children's home at the start of her life, but she had the idea that the world owed her something. However, that's not the way life works, as we all know.

In 2010, Nikki's mum received a letter from a solicitor saying that she had been left a lot of money in a will by her adopted parents — thousands of pounds. She got very excited and started making a list of all the things she was going to spend the money on.

At the same time, Nikki's brother had recently split up with his wife and had a new girlfriend. They came to see Nikki and me one night for a coffee. We all got on very well, but part of the conversation went back to Nikki's mum and dad. It wasn't anything bad or even related to them, but they took offence at it and demanded an apology from both of us. We refused because we hadn't said or done anything against them. As a result, they stopped speaking to Nikki and me. They even crossed to the other side of the street when we were out.

Nikki and I weren't particularly bothered by this, as it meant we no longer had to field the same everyday phone calls asking, "Hello, it's only me, where have you been? How have you been? What have you been doing?" After having the same conversation every day for over 20 years, it got a bit boring to say the least.

So, to Nikki and me, it was more of a relief when things went quiet between us and Nikki's mum and dad. However, now Nikki's brother had joined in and was taking sides with his mum and dad.

Now, Nikki and I are just getting on with our own lives. Towards the end of 2011, we went to Nikki's cousin's hairdressing salon for a haircut, and it was there that we found out that 35 years earlier, Nikki's mum had had a similar disagreement with Nikki's dad's wife. It was over something Nikki's mum didn't like, and they hadn't spoken since.

It all seemed very stupid. Life is too short, and there are enough problems in the world without adding more.

Chapter 30
The Loss of my Mum In 2012

Mum was getting on in years and had just celebrated her 99th birthday in 2012. She was becoming very frail and had Alzheimer's, but she was looking forward to receiving a telegram from the Queen on her 100th birthday next year.

Sadly, just one month after Mum's 99th birthday, she went to bed one night feeling very tired. As soon as her head hit the pillow, she fell asleep and didn't wake up. She died in her sleep that night. Both Hazel and Nicola were with her at the time, so at least she did not suffer. Mum was at peace.

The news of Mum's death filtered through the family all over the country, and we all learned of it on the same day it happened. I had been expecting this for some time. Over the last two or three years, Mum hadn't been in the best of health, but I didn't think it would come quite so soon. I had been thinking about it for a while, in fact, since Mum's 90th birthday. Back then, it seemed more likely that she would see her 100th or even live a little longer, as she was quite well then. But over the next nine years, her health slowly declined. I had been hoping that she would make it until next year or beyond if she were blessed with another year of life.

Mum wasn't to be so lucky. I had hoped she would see her 100th birthday as she so much wanted to receive the telegram from the Queen, but this wasn't to be.

I had been just about managing my finances for years, dealing with the debt left by ex-partners. From time to time, I had found myself in financial trouble, but I always managed to get out of it through a lot of perseverance. I wasn't the type to give up easily, even though I was close to doing so again. It would be around Christmas 2012 when I would finally be debt-free—for the last time.

If Mum had been blessed with just one more year of life, I would have been out of debt, and I had planned to stay that way for the rest of my life. I was getting close to retiring in just seven years and still had no money saved up.

I had no idea how I was going to find the money to attend Mum's funeral. I was still paying off my debts, which I would finish clearing by the end of the year. I was getting close to being at my wit's end, constantly asking myself how I was going to manage to get the money to go up for the funeral in just two weeks' time.

Then, in a last-ditch attempt, I came up with the idea of visiting the bank to see if I could get a higher overdraft than the £250 I already had on my account. When I explained what had happened, the bank said it was fine. They would let me have a larger overdraft of £500 to cover my travel costs, and I could pay it back, with no charges, within the next six months.

I decided that was the best course of action under the circumstances. It would put my plans back by a couple of months, but it didn't matter—the funeral was only five days away. It was a huge relief when the bank agreed.

Nikki and I still had our little Yorkshire Terrier, but this time, we couldn't take her with us. So, we asked a friend to look after her at home while we went up north for the funeral.

Nikki and I got ready for the long journey. This was the one journey I had been dreading for a long time—up to Darlington for the funeral. It would be nearly 400 miles from our home in Eastbourne to the northeast of England.

I had arranged with Kevin, my brother, and Andrew, my nephew, to travel in convoy up the motorways for the funeral. Andrew was now driving his own car, so the three cars would travel together as I didn't know where the hotel was that Kevin had booked.

The next day, I wasn't looking forward to driving all the way. This was the journey I had been dreading for months. I put the cases in the car, and we went down the road to Kevin's house, where we met Kevin and Marjorie. They weren't quite ready, so Nikki and I waited for a bit. As soon as it was time to go, we all got into our cars and set off for the next 8-10 hours.

The first part of our journey was about 70 miles to the other side of the Dartford Tunnel, where we stopped for about 35 minutes. Just as we were about to set off again, Marjorie looked horrified. She had just realised they had left their Salvation Army uniforms at home, over 70 miles away. Marjorie was in a panic.

"Oh my God, what are we going to do? It's too far to go all the way back home," she said. After some time, when Marjorie had calmed down and Kevin had considered the pros and cons of the situation, Andrew came up with the idea of going back on his own to Eastbourne for the uniforms and meeting us at Hazel's house in Darlington.

Kevin thought about it for a while and asked Andrew, "Are you sure you don't mind?" Marjorie reminded Kevin that Andrew drove for a living. Kevin then agreed, saying, "I know he does!" He turned to Andrew and said, "Okay, but drive carefully and don't go too fast, understand?" Andrew just nodded, raising his eyebrows as he walked back to his car.

We stayed for another coffee and loo break before continuing on our way. But before we went, Kevin wanted to drive for longer this time—at least four hours straight. I said I couldn't drive that long because I could only drive with one hand and needed to stop after a maximum of 2-3 hours.

Kevin's wife said that was fine, but I could see from Kevin's face that he wasn't very happy about it. However, he had to agree with his wife.

On the way up, I said to Nikki, "What is Kevin playing at? He keeps going behind Lorries doing only 60mph when we could be doing 70mph all the way. We'd get there a lot sooner if we did." I was getting quite annoyed about this but didn't say anything to Kevin.

At one point, 15 Lorries overtook us, and I didn't seem to be bothered about it. We had been driving this way for over 65 miles when, all of a sudden, Kevin overtook the lorry we had been following without indicating. A car that was just about to overtake us had to take evasive action to avoid causing an accident. We followed Kevin after the other car had gone past, and Kevin overtook 16 Lorries one after the other. I said to Nikki, "That's more like it. Now we're motoring!" Just as I said that, yes, you've guessed it, Kevin went behind a lorry and stayed there for the next 89 miles. I think that was to allow all the Lorries we had just overtaken to catch up. Ha!

We arrived at the lodge at 4:30 pm. By this time, I was getting very hungry, as I have diabetes and need to eat at regular times. But Kevin wanted to go straight to Hazel's. I was getting annoyed because it had gone way past mealtime. I had to eat, and that was that. Marjorie gave us Hazel's postcode to put in the satnav, as Kevin was insisting on going to Hazel's first so we could meet them there when we had eaten.

After we had eaten, we made our way to Hazel's house and parked just outside. We stayed for about two hours, then went back to the lodge and bed.

The next day, Nikki and I got up early and had a good English breakfast. Even though I wasn't supposed to have a fry-up, this was one time I was going to make an exception to the rule. I took Nikki into Darlington to show her where my old school was, to kill a bit of time, and a few other places where I had grown up during the first seven years of my life. The funeral wasn't until 2 pm, so we had a look at the covered market as well.

When Nikki and I arrived at Hazel's, we had to park just around the corner from her house. The neighbours were a bit funny about strangers parking in front of their driveways. I parked just off the driveway of a house, and the owners were just getting out of their car and gave me a funny look. I got out of my car, went around to the boot, and took out my black jacket. The people saw the black ribbon on the car aerial, and it was then they realised why we were there. Nothing more was said.

As Nikki and I walked just around the corner to Hazel's, I was nervous, but at the same time, I was there to pay my respects to a very special lady— the only mum I had ever known in my life. I was also hoping to see where my dad was buried at the same time.

We went into Hazel's and took our shoes off, as Hazel had a white carpet. But about half an hour later, we had to put them back on again when the funeral car arrived. We all went outside, and that's when I realised it was real—this was happening right here and now. My heart sank as I took a gulp and thought, *Mum's coffin had a Salvation Army flag over it, as a mark of respect for our Mum.*

Nikki and I got into the car behind the coffin for the long drive to the cemetery—or at least, that's what it felt like at the time. In the back of the car, I was thinking about the last time I saw my mum on her 90th birthday, now nine years ago, and how happy she was back then. But now it all seemed so surreal, like it wasn't happening, but it was.

It was very strange how the other drivers in Darlington gave way at all the junctions and roundabouts, while in Eastbourne, other road users wouldn't give way unless they had no choice.

When we arrived at the crematorium for the service, we had to wait outside for a while for Mum's coffin to be taken in. Then we all went in and sat down. I sat next to Kevin in the front row. I managed to hold the tears back almost to the end of the service, until Kevin started to cry. That started me off, but all the bad things that had happened in my life over the years had made me harder-hearted than Kevin. I still couldn't hold back the tears for long, though. As the coffin was lowered in front of us, I said to my mum, in my mind, *Goodbye, Mum, and God bless you for all eternity. Dad will be waiting for you up in Heaven.*

We all sang a song that Mum had written, but neither Kevin nor I could sing. We were both too upset to sing any more. Just after the last song, we all filed out of the crematorium. As we did, Hazel was holding on to both Kevin and me, saying that Mum was no longer in pain. She was back with Dad now and at peace. Nikki came over to me as we went towards the cars. I sparked up a fag and dragged the hell out of it, but felt better after that.

After a while, we got back into the cars and went back to the new Salvation Army Hall for coffee, just for an hour or so. Then we went back to the hotel to change and relax until the evening meeting. After the meeting, we all went for fish and chips. Nikki and I then went back to the hotel and bed, as we had an early start in the morning; we were going back on our own.

The next day came, and before we hit the road back home, we had a big cooked breakfast. Then we hit the road. The weather was very foggy that day, so to start with, I had to drive very carefully as we couldn't see more than two hundred yards in front of us. But after two hours on the road, the fog lifted, and I put my foot down. It wasn't long before we were doing 70 mph.

I overtook every lorry we came across on the road. Unlike Kevin on the way up, Nikki was a bit tense at first but soon got used to fast driving on the motorway. For a while, we had to slow down to 60 mph as the weather started to rain very hard. The heavens opened, and the surface water got quite bad for the next 80-odd miles. So, we stopped at a motorway services station for a long rest, as the last part of the journey would more than likely be the last part before home.

After a nice rest, we hit the road again. The weather had gone from rain to glorious sunshine, so I took advantage of the good weather and kept my foot down. It was 70 mph all the way home. It only took us 5.5 hours to get back, compared to the 8.5 hours it took to get to Darlington.

We were getting quite close to London now—just 80 miles to go before we hit the M25. I said to Nikki, "What do you think? Do you want to keep on going?"

Nikki replied, "It's up to you, you're the one driving."

I said I was just going to go for it all the way back home. It was only two more hours to go, so I just kept on driving until we got back home. Even though it was very tiring, all I could think of was that it wouldn't be long now. As the miles got fewer, I knew we were getting closer to home.

When we arrived back home, the dog went bonkers. We weren't surprised, but the good thing was that the dog had been very good.

I was knackered after all that driving, and we went to bed early and slept in the next day, which didn't matter as I didn't have to go back to work until the day after that.

Love & God Bless. R.I.P.

The End

No matter what comes your way in life—
Good, bad, or the sad times—

Always look on the bright side of life,
And things will get better for you.

So be happy with yourself, and life will be good to you.

The Author of this book, is K. Rareheart

And then the story continues with

Book 2: In My Mind

A look into his experiences, the ups and downs

Of his life, the stress he faced,

And how he kept on top of things.

www.ingramcontent.com/pod-product-compliance
Lightning Source LLC
Chambersburg PA
CBHW050233120526
44590CB00016B/2074